Also by Natasha D. Frazier

<u>Devotionals</u>

The Life Your Spirit Craves

Not Without You

<u>Fiction</u>

Love, Lies & Consequences

Through Thick & Thin: Love, Lies & Consequences Book 2

Copyright © 2016 by Natasha D. Frazier
Published by Encouraging Works
Printed by Lightning Source, Inc.

All rights reserved. No portion of this book may be used in any form without the written permission of the publisher.

Printed in the United States of America.

ISBN: 978-0-9884521-8-3

Scripture quotations are NLT unless otherwise noted. Scripture quotations marked NLT are taken from the Holy
Bible, New Living Translation, copyright © 1996, 2004.
Used by permission of Tyndale House Publishers, Inc.,
Carol Stream, Illinois 60188. All rights reserved.

Edited by: Cheryl Molin

Cover design by BJ Benjamin O'Neal (I Imagine Beyond)

For Order Information, please visit:
www.natashafrazier.com

Note from the Author

I cannot publish any book without giving thanks to my Heavenly Father, who has been so loving and faithful to me. He has blessed me with the heart to encourage women and the ability to do that through writing. Thank you for entrusting me with such a task. He has also given me a wonderful family who supports my writing career. Eddie, my awesome husband, I love you and appreciate you for all that you do. Thank you for your unwavering support. Eden, Ethan & Emilyn, I do believe that aside from God, you all made this book possible. Every day with you all teaches me a spiritual lesson. Mommy loves each of you so much. (Emilyn- even though you aren't here just yet, I'm sure you will continue to add to the lessons learned.) Mommy! Thank you for your unconditional love and support from afar. You make sure that everyone knows that your baby is an author. Thank you! Courtney, Amber, Dad, General Lee, and to the rest of my family, I love you and thank you.

To my special set of girlfriends who push me to go further and have encouraged me from the very start: Tiera, Toccara & Shenitra - I love you ladies and appreciate your friendship.

To the fabulous mommies out there - You each hold a special place in my heart. My prayer is that God continues to strengthen you in your parenting journey and that you find it joyful and rewarding most days. (smile) I hope that this book inspires you to take a look at your own lives and see how God is present each and every day. And to my readers and supporters, I appreciate the love and all that you do!

Much love & many blessings,

Natasha

Dedicated to Eden, Ethan & Emilyn

The Life Your Spirit Craves for Mommies:

52-week Devotional and Journal

NATASHA D. FRAZIER

Week 1 - Just Because You Cannot See

"This is my command—be strong and courageous! Do not be afraid or discouraged. For the Lord your God is with you wherever you go." (Joshua 1:9)

We were riding in two separate cars, my husband in his car and the kids and me in the other. We had just left Firestone, paying for the repairs on my husband's vehicle, and were on our way back home. It was late in the evening. My daughter had taken a short nap that day, but apparently it wasn't enough because she was relatively cranky. Everything bothered her and she whined and questioned continually.

During the drive home, she whined and constantly asked where her daddy was. I kept telling her that he was right behind us; he left immediately after we did. After going through this series of the same questions and same responses about ten times, she said, "I can't see him" and then continued to whine more. I reminded her, "Just because you cannot see him doesn't mean he isn't there!" My frustration was beginning to match hers.

Somewhere in my agitation at her constant whining, the Lord reminded me of His Presence. "Natasha, just because you cannot see Me doesn't mean I am not here." My moment of agitation with her immediately shifted to God's patience with me.

I'm sure I am not the only one who sometimes get frustrated when things aren't going the way I think they should go, and not the only one to wonder exactly where God is and how He is going to work the situation out. Just because we cannot physically see Him doesn't mean He isn't there.

Has there been an area of your life where it seems that God is not present? An unanswered prayer, perhaps? I encourage you to take a few moments and meditate on today's Scripture and to think back over the area where you feel He isn't there. You will likely find that He is present but not in the way that you have expected.

Prayer: Heavenly Father, thank You for always being present in my life, even when it doesn't feel like it. Whenever I'm feeling alone and in need of more of You, please remind me that You are forever with me. In Jesus' name, Amen.

Further study: John 14:16; Deuteronomy 31:6

The Life Your Spirit Craves for Mommies

Week 1 - Journal

~

Have you ever felt like God was not present in your life? If so, what was going on in your life to make you feel this way?

_____
_____
_____
_____
_____
_____
_____
_____

Take a moment to think about times when you were certain of God's presence in your life. Write a couple of them down here to refer back to when things get hectic.

_____
_____
_____
_____
_____
_____
_____
_____

How do the scriptures for this week encourage you in the fact that God is always there?

_____
_____
_____
_____
_____
_____
_____

Natasha D. Frazier

Week 2 - Let Me Wipe Your Tears

"Dear friends, since God loved us that much, we surely ought to love each other." (1 John 4:11)

Lately, my mornings have not been going as planned. The general plan is to dress myself and then wake my children to get them ready. Since we're totally off track, my children get out of bed before I'm ready, thus slowing us down and usually adding chaos to our morning routine.

My toddler is on a path to get into everything that he shouldn't. This particular morning, he was going through my bathroom cabinet space pulling out my feather comb. Problem with this is that the handle is long with a pointy end. Of course I took it away several times, but the final time, he couldn't take it anymore. He had a fit! A stream of tears and an extremely pouty face followed.

In the midst of that, my daughter did something that surprised and encouraged me. She sat down on the bathroom floor next to him and said, "Let me wipe your tears," and proceeded to do just that. To my amazement, he stopped crying. In that moment, the Holy Spirit nudged me. We should show that kind of love to the people in our lives. Loving them through their pain instead of judging them. Sometimes all it takes is a listening ear and someone to *wipe away the tears.* Whose tears can you wipe today?

Prayer: Heavenly Father, give me a heart that is loving and pure. Help me not to be judgmental but to show the kind of love that pleases You and encourages those You place in my path. In Jesus' name, Amen.

Further study: 1 John 4:7–21

The Life Your Spirit Craves for Mommies

Week 2 - Journal

~

When is the last time you provided a listening ear to someone who needed it?

_____
_____
_____
_____
_____
_____
_____
_____
_____

Has God ever placed you in a position to wipe away someone else's tears? How did you respond?

_____
_____
_____
_____
_____
_____
_____
_____

Pray and ask God to show you if there is someone in your life now who could use your loving shoulder and listening ears. Write your prayer here.

_____
_____
_____
_____
_____
_____
_____
_____

Natasha D. Frazier

Week 3 - Pray About Everything

"Never stop praying." (1 Thessalonians 5:17)

My daughter has a heart for prayer. Before dinner, she asks to say prayer before we eat. Funny thing is that she often prays about everything but dinner, and my husband or I will have to interject and remind her to give thanks for the food on the table.

Her prayers range from giving thanks that she's going to kindergarten to thanking God for her toys or her brother or her friends in her class. She will thank God for the cups, plates, utensils, juice, and stove. Recently, we had a storm come through that caused us to lose power. Ever since then, she's thanked God for the power and for a working TV, refrigerator, stove, etc.

My husband and I joke about her long prayers that have nothing to do with the occasion (dinner), but there is something to be said for her heart and the faith of a child. As adults we take so many things for granted, but what if we truly prayed to God about everything? What if we had faith as a child? Believing that God hears us? Trusting in His character without the cares of life clouding our faith?

As I challenge myself, I challenge you to take everything to God in prayer today and trust Him without question. Even though God is all knowing, I do believe He wants to be invited into every area of our lives. Will you join me in drawing closer to God through prayer?

Prayer: Heavenly Father, thank You for the life lessons that You teach us through our children. As I draw nearer to You today by pouring out my heart, I trust and believe that You care for me and are drawing me closer to You. Teach me to truly bring everything to You in prayer and to pray without ceasing. In Jesus' name, Amen.

Further study: 1 Thessalonians 5:16–18

The Life Your Spirit Craves for Mommies

Week 3 - Journal

~

Have you ever felt like a situation was too small to take to God in prayer? What was it? If so, take a moment and give your "small" thing to God.

_____
_____
_____
_____
_____

Have you prayed about something that you thought was small and God answered your prayer in a major way? Take a moment and write it here as a reminder to yourself that God cares about everything concerning you.

_____
_____
_____
_____
_____
_____
_____
_____
_____
_____
_____

What hinders you from taking everything to God in prayer? Write a prayer asking God to remove that hindrance and give you a heart to pray about everything.

_____
_____
_____
_____
_____
_____
_____

Natasha D. Frazier

Week 4 - Praying with Expectancy

"Keep on asking, and you will receive what you ask for. Keep on seeking, and you will find. Keep on knocking, and the door will be opened to you. For everyone who asks, receives. Everyone who seeks, finds. And to everyone who knocks, the door will be opened." (Matthew 7:7–8)

How persistent are you? How many times do you ask God for something? Do you ask once and then leave it alone? Do you ask continuously? You should keep asking until your prayers are answered. I think that children are the most determined when it comes to getting what they want. Children will continue to ask their parents for something until they receive it. Sometimes the parent's answer is "later," "maybe," or "not yet." It may even be "no." However, many children still maintain a tenacious and expectant spirit.

A recent example of this is my daughter requesting eight dollars for a special lunch that's offered at her school on Fridays. I swear she would not let me forget about those eight dollars. Every day, she asked until she received. She made her request known. There was no doubt about what she wanted and she made sure both of her parents knew it. There are a couple of things to note here: (1) she knew the source and (2) she believed that her source would provide what she was asking.

With the same spirit, we should continue to seek God because He is our source. He instructs us to keep on seeking, keep on asking, and keep on knocking. In doing this, we are obedient to His Word and we demonstrate that we believe He will answer our prayers. However, don't let your prayers simply become about asking God to open doors for you. God is more concerned with hearing from us, so He desires that we continue to seek Him, even if in all of our persistence His answer is no.

Prayer: Heavenly Father, thank You for Your faithfulness. Keep me determined, faithful, and keep me from becoming weary when seeking You. Give me perseverance and strength as I wait on You. In Jesus' name, Amen.

Further study: Matthew 7:7–10

The Life Your Spirit Craves for Mommies

Week 4 - Journal

~

Do you sometimes get tired of praying about the same thing? Why? Is it because you believe that God already knows and there is no need for you to pray about it continually? Do you feel like you're bothering God?

_____
_____
_____
_____
_____
_____

Do you believe that if you continually pray about a specific situation that God will eventually answer you? (Even if the answer is *no*)

_____
_____
_____
_____

Though God desires that we pray with expectancy and continually, do you use your prayer time as an opportunity to grow closer to God?

_____
_____
_____
_____

If there has been something you've been praying and believing God for, by faith, write a prayer of thanksgiving for His answer.

_____
_____
_____
_____
_____

Natasha D. Frazier

Week 5 - Always There

I can never escape from your Spirit! I can never get away from your presence! If I go up to heaven, you are there; if I go down to the grave, you are there. (Psalm 139:7-8)

On several occasions, I have muddled through my purse to search for something, only to find a toy or half-eaten snack that belongs to one of my children. Or I have simply placed a hand in a jacket pocket for comfort, and felt something else that belonged to one of them. Purse, car, or any other place that they've been, generally something in it reminds me that they've been around. These little reminders of them put a smile on my face, reminding me of the joy that comes with being their mommy.

God is everywhere and He often lets us know this in little ways as well. It could be a prayer that you've whispered to Him. He shows He is there and He listens by confirming that through a conversation or a sermon at church. An answered request of which you've mentioned to no one but Him. Maybe you've had a rough day and He sends someone along to encourage you. Or a song on the radio speaks to your heart at just the right moment.

It is such a joyful time when we experience God's little reminders. No matter where we are or what we're up to, He is always there. There is no place that we can go that He is not. There is no greater joy in knowing that God is omnipresent and that He is constantly proving that and His love for us.

Prayer: Father in Heaven, I feel an unexplainable joy in receiving reminders from You, knowing that You are forever with me and that You love me. Thank You for the ways in which You show that You care. Even in knowing everything about me, You still love me and have chosen me for Your purpose. I am eternally grateful and will forever praise Your Holy name. In Jesus' name, Amen.

Further study: Psalm 139

The Life Your Spirit Craves for Mommies

Week 5 - Journal

~

Do you generally notice little reminders from God? What reminders has God left for you lately?

_____
_____
_____
_____
_____
_____
_____
_____
_____

For your future reference, take some time this week and jot down any reminders of God's presence in your life. Remember that He is always there.

_____
_____
_____
_____
_____
_____
_____
_____
_____
_____

What did you learn about God after studying Psalm 139?

_____
_____
_____
_____
_____

Natasha D. Frazier

Week 6 - The Golden Rule

"Do to others as you would like them to do to you." (Luke 6:31)

The Golden Rule! Christ's simple statement was plastered all over my grade-school classrooms. We teach this rule to our children but sometimes forget it when we become adults. There are no exceptions to this rule. For example, it doesn't mean to only treat those we love in the same manner as you would like to be treated. You and I are to deal with everyone in the same way we desire to be regarded.

It is easy to love those who love you in return. The challenge is being kind to the person who doesn't like you, despises you, or wants nothing to do with you. Consider the coworker who never greets you in return, the rude family member or the nasty retail associate; you should apply the golden rule to them as well. This is how you truly let the love of God shine through you.

It doesn't matter whether you know someone personally or if you even like them, you should always treat them the way you want to be treated. The love you show them just may be the love that they need. Some people don't know how to deal with personal problems, so everyone they come into contact with suffers.

As you move throughout your day, choose to be kind to all who you come into contact with regardless of their disposition. God desires that you love everyone, even the unlovable. This is how we teach our children—by being the example—because our children are always watching and imitating our every move.

Prayer: Heavenly Father, sometimes it is hard for me to treat others the same way I want to be treated. Help me to look past the nasty behavior of difficult people and show them the same level of love and courtesy that I desire. In Jesus' name, Amen.

Further study: Luke 6:27–36

The Life Your Spirit Craves for Mommies

Week 6 - Journal

~

Do you sometimes have a difficult time applying the Golden Rule in situations where you deem the other person should not be given the same consideration? (ex. This could be because this person may have a terrible attitude.)

_____
_____
_____
_____
_____
_____
_____

Do you often treat others as you want to be treated? Why or why not?

_____
_____
_____
_____
_____
_____
_____
_____
_____
_____

Has your child ever witnessed you applying (or not) the Golden rule in a situation where it was difficult? How did you use that as a teachable moment?

_____
_____
_____
_____
_____
_____
_____
_____
_____

Natasha D. Frazier

Week 7 - The Father's Love

"So if you sinful people know how to give good gifts to your children, how much more will your heavenly Father give the Holy Spirit to those who ask Him." (Luke 11:13)

Becoming a parent helps put things in perspective when it comes to love. The love that parents have for their children is immeasurable. Parents love their children so much that they will do anything for them and strive to provide the best for them. Parents desire to give children everything they need, and even the things they want when suitable.

You can identify with the love of a parent because of your love for your child(ren). Now consider our Father in Heaven. He is much greater and more powerful than we are. His love for us far exceeds the love that we have for our own children. When I consider how much I love my children, I am overwhelmed thinking about how much more God loves me!

The Holy Spirit is the best gift that God gives us next to salvation. God gives us what we need, and all that we need is wrapped up in the Holy Spirit. The Holy Spirit gives us direction, comfort, peace, and so much more. Through the Holy Spirit, God gives what we ask when it is in our best interest and in alignment with His will.

Trust and know today that God provides His best for you, as a parent does for his child, and that His way is perfect.

Prayer: Heavenly Father, thank You for being the ultimate parent. Thank You for loving me beyond measure and doing what will bring Your name glory. I find comfort in knowing that Your ways are perfect and Your gifts to me are far greater than anything I can imagine. In Jesus' name, Amen.

Further study: Luke 11:9–13

The Life Your Spirit Craves for Mommies

Week 7 - Journal

~

Take a moment to think about how much you love your child(ren). Now take a moment to think about how much more God loves you. Write a prayer of thanksgiving for God's love.

_____
_____
_____
_____
_____
_____
_____
_____

When you consider how much God loves you, is there any room for doubt as to if He will take care of you? Answer your prayers?

_____
_____
_____
_____
_____
_____

If you've been questioning whether or not God is going to answer a prayer, I encourage you to write that prayer down here with the understanding and faith to believe that He can and will do exceedingly and abundantly more than you would do for your own child; therefore, consider it taken care of.

_____
_____
_____
_____
_____
_____

Natasha D. Frazier

Week 8 - No Good Thing

"For the Lord God is our sun and our shield. He gives us grace and glory. The Lord will withhold no good thing from those who do what is right." (Psalm 84:11)

Can you recall asking your parents for something that you thought was good for you and becoming upset because you did not receive it, only to later realize that it really wasn't the best thing for you? As a parent, I have often withheld certain things from my children. It may be that extra piece of candy or a gift purchased that was out of their age range, so it's spending time on the closet shelf. Because of my children's ages, they likely won't understand the reasoning behind my choices, but hopefully one day they will.

The Bible tells us that the Lord is our sun. The sun illuminates our path and gives us direction. The Lord is also our shield, which protects us from the evils of this world. He gives us what we do not deserve when He gives us grace.

He seeks to give us good things when we are blameless before Him. Our belief in Christ's death and resurrection is what makes us righteous. We cannot be righteous on our own. We will not always do what is right, but God is merciful. When we slip and fall, we should get back up and try again. God in all of His infinite wisdom knows what is good for us and will give it to us.

As you go throughout your day, remember that God gives direction, protection and grace. He will also give you good things in due season. So if you desire something from God today, know that He doesn't withhold any good thing from His children, just as you wouldn't keep any good thing from your own children. Be patient, wait on Him, and trust in His knowledge because He knows whether or not what you want is good for you.

Prayer: Heavenly Father, thank You for being who You are: faithful and powerful. Thank You for not withholding any good thing from me. I trust that all that You give to me is good, and I only want Your good gifts and what You desire to give me. In Jesus' name, Amen.

Further study: Psalm 84

The Life Your Spirit Craves for Mommies

Week 8 - Journal

~

Think about your relationship with your child(ren). Consider reasons why you would withhold good things from them. Maybe they're immature. Perhaps they're not ready. Or possibly, it just isn't the right time or season for that thing.

_____
_____
_____
_____
_____
_____
_____

Is there something weighing heavily on your heart that you've been pleading with God about? Is it good for you? Based on your answers to the above questions, could one of those reasons be the same reason why you haven't received what you've been asking for?

_____
_____
_____
_____
_____
_____
_____

Write a prayer thanking God for His wisdom in knowing when to release His good things to you. Ask that He gives you patience as you wait for His timing.

_____
_____
_____
_____
_____
_____
_____

Natasha D. Frazier

Week 9 - Be Transformed

"Don't copy the behavior and customs of this world, but let God transform you into a new person by changing the way you think. Then you will learn to know God's will for you, which is good and pleasing and perfect." (Romans 12:2)

Have you ever had an issue with your child wanting to fit in or be like someone else in class? Perhaps you see your child not just wanting to be somewhat like them, but going as far to duplicate their behavior. If so, do you remember trying to teach them why they shouldn't be copying someone else?

As children of God, we should want to learn and live God's will for our lives. However, we cannot accomplish this if we continue to straddle the fence and desire to live as though we do not know God. We shouldn't talk like people of the world, treat our enemies like people of the world do, or even attempt to blend in with people of the world. We should be different because God has set us apart. People should be able to look at God's children and take note that something is peculiar about them.

To live a changed life, we must first transform our thoughts. We cannot do this on our own; therefore, we must allow God to change our thought patterns. God does this through His Word and prayer. We have to consistently spend time in His Word, because what we put into our spirit is what we will get out. If we're constantly feeding our spirit things that are holy and pure, our thoughts will become the same, which is what God desires.

Once our thoughts are transformed, then we will be able to learn God's will for us. Only then will we live the life that God has called us to live, pleasing Him and doing His will. God's will propels us into destiny, gives Him glory, and elevates His people. Let the Lord transform your mind today so that you can do what you have been created to do.

Prayer: Heavenly Father, thank You for Your will that has been predetermined for me. Today, I commit to allowing You to change my mind and my thoughts so that they may be pleasing to You. In Jesus' name, Amen.

Further study: Romans 12:1–2 and Philippians 4:8–9

The Life Your Spirit Craves for Mommies

Week 9 - Journal

~

Have you had an issue with your child copying the behavior of someone else? How did you handle it?

_____
_____
_____
_____
_____
_____
_____

Have you ever found yourself trying to fit in with those around you? If so, why were you trying to fit in? Did you find yourself compromising your relationship with God to fit in? What was the result?

_____
_____
_____
_____
_____
_____
_____
_____
_____
_____
_____
_____

Whether or not this is something that you still deal with, write a prayer asking God to help you stand firm in His word and what you know to be true. Commit to allowing God's word to change your mind, your heart and your thoughts.

_____
_____
_____
_____

Natasha D. Frazier

Week 10 - God Gives Authority

Everyone must submit to governing authorities. For all authority comes from God, and those in positions of authority have been placed there by God." (Romans 13:1)

As parents, God has given us authority over our children. When we think about the order of the household and how things are supposed to work, we know that things don't work well when someone is out of order, in this case, disobedient children.

God has also given us governing authorities in government, churches, and workplaces to keep order and honor Him. He has chosen those whom He desires to be authority figures, and as children of God, we must respect that. We often have issues with the way the president runs the country, the pastor and elders lead the church, our managers supervise their employees, and husbands lead their households. However, we should not allow our issues with authorities to cause us to disrespect them.

Just as we expect our children to learn to treat us with respect, love, and obedience, we must respect those in authority as God's leaders and treat them the way that God wants us to treat them. When we submit to proper authority, we are able to have a clear mind because we have done what we're supposed to do.

In any area of life where you have an issue with those in authority, do not allow your issues to cause you to sin by being disrespectful. The Bible warns us that when we rebel against authority, we are rebelling against God, because He has placed them in those positions.

Prayer: Heavenly Father, thank You for the governing authorities that You've given us in every area of life to help keep order. Let me treat them with love and respect as You have said in Your Word. Help me to give honor to those to whom it is due just as I expect love and obedience in my household. In Jesus' name, Amen.

Further study: Romans 13:1–7

The Life Your Spirit Craves for Mommies

Week 10 - Journal

~

Do you sometimes have an issue with those in authority? Why?

_____
_____
_____
_____

Does knowing what God's word says about those in authority have an impact on how you see those in authority in your life? Why or why not?

_____
_____
_____
_____
_____
_____

If you have issues with authority figures, do you notice your children encountering the same issues? If so, how do you handle it?

_____
_____
_____
_____
_____
_____

Study Romans 13:1-7. Write a prayer asking God to help you honor and respect those in authority because He placed them there.

_____
_____
_____
_____

Natasha D. Frazier

Week 11 - Again and Again

"Repeat them again and again to your children. Talk about them when you are at home and when you are on the road, when you are going to bed and when you are getting up." (Deuteronomy 6:7)

A task that you want your child to learn. The ABC song. Nursery rhymes. They all have one thing in common: repetition. It is easy to learn nearly anything when you practice it often. The Word of God says that we will enjoy long life, success, and all that God has promised when we keep His Word in our hearts and obey it. How do we keep His Word hidden in our hearts so that it may come to our remembrance when we need it? Repetition!

We have to continuously keep the Word of God before us. God's Word says to talk about it all the time, day and night, at home and away from home, and to our children. It is so easy to slip into unholy conversation. We should instead strive to keep the Word of God in our mouths, strengthening ourselves and those around us. God's Word is refreshing and life changing. It's like holding up a mirror so that one can see himself just as he is and submit to God for cleansing.

Choose to talk about the Word of God and His promises today. Give Him praise and keep your heart and mind focused on Him so that you can be sure to do all that He has called you to do. Be intentional in serving God wholeheartedly today.

Prayer: Heavenly Father, thank You for Your Word that gives my spirit life. Keep Your Word on my mind today so that my focus may remain on You. Keep Your Word in my mouth today so that I may encourage others and myself to walk along the path that You have designed. In Jesus' name, Amen.

Further study: Deuteronomy 6

The Life Your Spirit Craves for Mommies

Week 11 - Journal

~

What is the last thing you taught your child(ren) through the act of repetition?

_____
_____
_____
_____
_____
_____

What is the last thing that you've learned through the act of repetition? (It is important to know that some things are learned through habit whether good or bad.)

_____
_____
_____
_____
_____

What would happen if you applied those same techniques toward improving your relationship with God?

_____
_____
_____
_____
_____

Is there an area of your life that you'd like to improve? Write it here along with a plan of how you will improve it. Remember that your actions need to be consistent, repetitious (to develop a habit) and in alignment with God's Word.

_____
_____
_____
_____
_____

Week 12 - What are you searching for?

If you search for good, you will find favor, but if you search for evil, it will find you!" (Proverbs 11:27)

When I was a child, my mother frequently warned that if I went looking for trouble, I would find it. It was true then and it's true now. Whatever we set our sights on and seek, that is what we will find. Because of this truth, we need to intentionally seek the good in all things.

We must seek the good in people, circumstances, and even in ourselves. When we search for the good in others, we usually see them differently than the way others see them. As believers, God sees who we are or should be in Christ, rather than seeing our sins. When we choose to love others and see them as God sees them, I believe we are treating them the way God would want us to treat them. Don't be quick to judge. Seeking the good in circumstances allows us to keep an open mind, remain optimistic, and see the up side of things. We shape a positive perspective. When we seek the good in ourselves, we are moved to give the best of ourselves.

As you go through your day, remain positive and look at people and situations through the lens of the Holy Spirit.

Prayer: Heavenly Father, thank You for Your Word. Help me to always search for good so that I may find favor. Help me to see life through the lens of the Holy Spirit. In Jesus' name, Amen.

Further study: Proverbs 11

The Life Your Spirit Craves for Mommies

Week 12 - Journal

~

Throughout this week, intentionally seek the positive side of every situation. Journal how this changed your perspective.

_____
_____
_____
_____
_____
_____
_____
_____
_____
_____

Think about a current situation and consider how you're looking at it. Does your perspective change if you look at it the way God would see it?

_____
_____
_____
_____
_____

Is there something about yourself or your children that you perceive in a negative light? How would God see it? Write a prayer asking God to open your heart to help you see this the way He does.

_____
_____
_____
_____
_____
_____

Week 13 - Purposed to Please

"For we speak as messengers approved by God to be entrusted with the Good News. Our purpose is to please God, not people. He alone examines the motives of our hearts." (1 Thessalonians 2:4)

Some of us are people pleasers. We want to be liked by everyone; we want to fit in; so we do what we can to please others. When asked to take on a task, even if our schedules are already overloaded, we say yes because we are afraid of people not liking us. This behavior starts when we're children because we want to please our parents, teachers and others in authority; unfortunately, some of us never grow out of this stage.

People pleasers tend to be *nice*. They often want to say or do something contrary to what they're actually doing, but since their focus is on pleasing others, they do what they think others want them to do.

We have to realize that we will never be able to please everyone and there will be people who won't like us. That is okay, because ultimately the only one we should be aiming to please is the Lord. We have to remember that we were created for His purpose, and not the purpose someone else has determined for us. As Paul says in today's Scripture, "Our purpose is to please God, not people."

We need to get in alignment with our purpose and begin to do what pleases the Lord. What pleases the Lord will not always please people, and as children of God who are seeking to become all that we were created to be, we have to be okay with that. God has a much higher calling for our lives than to be worried about who likes us.

Prayer: Heavenly Father, thank You for Your life-changing holy Word. I am thankful that I only have to live to please You. Help me to remain mindful of that and keep You as the center of my life. In Jesus' name, Amen.

Further study: 1 Thessalonians 2:1–16

The Life Your Spirit Craves for Mommies

Week 13 - Journal

~

Are you a people pleaser? If so, why do you feel the need to have the approval of others? Why is this important to you?

_____
_____
_____
_____
_____
_____
_____
_____
_____

Is having the approval of people more important than having God's approval?

_____
_____
_____
_____
_____

What have you done to shift from being a people pleaser to a God pleaser?

_____
_____
_____
_____
_____
_____
_____
_____

Has the issue of people pleasing kept you from doing something that you know God has called you to do? If so, write a prayer asking God to help you to walk in your purpose, which is to please Him. Ask for courage and strength to move forward whether or not you have the approval of others.

The Life Your Spirit Craves for Mommies

Week 14 - Divine Discipline

"No discipline is enjoyable while it is happening—it's painful! But afterward there will be a peaceful harvest of right living for those who are trained in this way." (Hebrews 12:11)

Parents discipline their children to instill values in them, teach them right from wrong, and help them develop good character. Children are disciplined when they disobey their parents and decide to do what they think is right or simply choose what is more pleasurable.

The Lord is our spiritual parent and will also discipline us when we choose a path different from the one He has predestined for us. Disobedience warrants discipline. The Lord disciplines us because He loves us and wants the best for us— His will. Just as earthly parents discipline their children to get them back on track, so does the Lord.

We must remember that divine discipline is a consequence for our disobedience and must not allow it to discourage us. We should take it in stride and note that God loves us, is looking out for us, and desires that discipline will put us back on the right path. Divine discipline is supposed to produce holy living.

When the Lord puts you in time-out, delays a treat, or spiritually spanks you, remember that it is for your spiritual growth; allow it to redirect you to where you should be.

Prayer: Heavenly Father, thank You for divine discipline. Help me to remember that it is for my spiritual development so that I can become who You want me to be. In Jesus' name, Amen.

Further study: Hebrews 12:1–13

Week 14 - Journal

~

Do you view chastisement from the Lord as a form of love? Why or Why not?

Can you recall a time when you were recently spiritually disciplined? Did it help you grow as a Christian?

Do you weigh the consequences of sin or God's divine discipline before choosing whether or not to be obedient? Why or why not?

The Life Your Spirit Craves for Mommies

_____
_____

There are obviously situations when we don't have time to weigh our options; this is why it's important that the Word of God and His ways are embedded in our hearts. Write a prayer asking God to give you a heart that is sensitive to His voice in order that you will sin less against Him and choose what is right in His sight.

_____
_____
_____
_____
_____
_____
_____
_____
_____
_____

Natasha D. Frazier

Week 15 - Listeners and Doers

"But don't just listen to God's word. You must do what it says. Otherwise, you are only fooling yourselves." (James 1:22)

When my kids mess up, I take a moment and explain to them that what they did was wrong and why it was wrong. I always end my speeches with "Do you understand me?" In response, I always receive a "Yes, ma'am." Whether or not they understand, it doesn't always show. Often they repeat their actions or do something along the same lines; that says to me that they're simply going to do what they want to do and suffer the consequences later. This is a terrible line of thinking that seems to follow us into adulthood and interferes with us doing what God's Word says, even when we know what He requires of us.

In order to develop a character and lifestyle that brings honor to God, we must allow His Word to direct us. We have to decide to live according to His Word, but we cannot do this if we don't know what it says. So many of us attend weekly services but fail to live a life that is pleasing to God because we only listen to God's Word. We don't retain it, and so we don't put it into practice.

We must get to a place in our relationship with God where we long for His presence, desire to please Him, and choose His ways. Obedience and love are two of God's most important requirements for His children. We honor God when we obey His holy Word. It is then that we will begin to experience the abundant life that He has promised His children.

Like children, we often want the blessings of God but we don't want to abide by His Word. This isn't the way things work, and our disobedience is cause for many delayed blessings. As God's children, we must wholeheartedly devote ourselves to Him and choose to follow His Word without exception. Choose to move from only listening to the Word of God to learning and living it.

Prayer: Heavenly Father, I give praise to Your holy name. Help me to receive, accept, learn, and apply Your Word to my life in all circumstances. Help me to show my love for You by being obedient. In Jesus' name, Amen.

Further study: James 1:19–27

The Life Your Spirit Craves for Mommies

Week 15 - Journal

~

What do you think is your biggest barrier to studying and retaining God's word in your heart?

_____
_____
_____
_____
_____
_____

Do you ever make decisions to do what you want to do and suffer the consequences later? Why do you choose to put yourself in such situations for temporary gratification?

_____
_____
_____
_____
_____
_____
_____
_____
_____

For the next few days, meditate on James 1:19-27. Does it encourage you to want to be a better Christian?

_____
_____
_____
_____
_____
_____
_____
_____

Natasha D. Frazier

Week 16 - Rejection and Disobedience

"They stumble because they do not obey God's word, and so they meet the fate that was planned for them." (1 Peter 2:8b)

How many times have you instructed your children not to do a certain thing and they did it anyway? For me, probably more times than I can count. I suppose it is all a part of their learning process, but when they are disobedient, the result is the same: pain. The same is true for us when we choose not to live according to God's Word.

We reject God when we're disobedient, and as a result, we stumble. As long as we choose not to adhere to God's holy Word, we will continue to stumble. We often make excuses and attempt to choose which Scriptures we want to obey, but God is not pleased. If there were Scriptures that He didn't intend for us to abide by, His Word would say so.

Being obedient to God's Word is not always going to feel good or please our flesh, but that is not the intent. We obey God to honor Him and live in a way that pleases Him. We are His creation, so we must do what we were created to do. We often want to be obedient when it is convenient for us or when we want God to answer our prayers. If we can choose to be obedient then, we can choose to follow Him at all times.

As you go through your day, remember that you are faced with a choice. Obedience is a decision. We know the results of disobedience and that is our fate when we choose it: pain. Today I encourage you to choose to show others the goodness of the Lord by living as an obedient child of God.

Prayer: Heavenly Father, I praise You. I know the consequences of my sin, so let me be reminded of that when I am faced with a choice to obey You or my selfish desires. I truly want to please You. In Jesus' name, Amen.

Further study: 1 Peter 2:4–12 and 1 Peter 4:1–1

The Life Your Spirit Craves for Mommies

Week 16 - Journal

~

We reject God when we're disobedient, and as a result, we stumble. Do you view your disobedience as rejecting God? If not, would viewing your sin as rejecting God affect the decisions you make?

_____
_____
_____
_____
_____

We often want to be obedient when it is convenient for us or when we want God to answer our prayers. Are you guilty of being on your *best behavior* when you're waiting on God to answer a prayer?

_____
_____
_____
_____

Obedience is a decision. Make a conscious decision to be obedient this week. Choose a couple of situations that you encountered this week and write the results of you choosing God's way over your own. Would you like to see these results all the time?

_____
_____
_____
_____
_____
_____
_____
_____
_____

Natasha D. Frazier

Week 17 - The Lord Requires More of You

"He has shown you, O mortal, what is good. And what does the Lord require of you? To act justly and to love mercy and to walk humbly with your God." (Micah 6:8 NIV)

The Holy Spirit speaks to me a lot when I'm dealing with my children. As I interact with them, I'm often reminded of how much more loving God is to me. He is so much more patient with me when I'm not acting the way that I should.

If you have children, you know how most two-year-olds are. Stubborn! I can recall many times when my daughter was two and I would try to get her to do something and she didn't cooperate. One particular day, I was asking her to pick something up off the floor. She continued to be stubborn with her usual *no's* and *I did it already*. After ignoring my instructions, she asked for a snack and to watch Disney Jr. I reminded her: "You cannot continue to be disobedient and expect to get what you ask for all the time!" Immediately, it was as if I heard the Lord repeating those exact same words to me. Ouch! However, He reminded me of His faithfulness and mercy to me even when I don't deserve it.

Oftentimes, we are not being the person whom God has called us to be, yet we continue to ask Him to bless us and do all of these things for us. Although God sometimes grants our requests when we haven't done what we're supposed to do, our Scripture today reminds us of what God requires. God wants our obedience; so let's remember to check ourselves to make sure that we're doing all that God has called us to do. As you go about your day, seek to be obedient. Think about how faithful and kind the Lord is to you even when you don't deserve it.

Prayer: Heavenly Father, thank You for Your faithfulness and kindness even when I am unfaithful. Teach me to act justly, love mercy, and walk humbly with You. In Jesus' name, Amen.

Further study: Micah 6

The Life Your Spirit Craves for Mommies

Week 17 - Journal

~

Think of God's faithfulness to you. Write about a time when God has shown you favor even when you didn't deserve it.

_____
_____
_____
_____
_____
_____
_____
_____
_____
_____

Does studying Micah 6:8 encourage you to be obedient?

_____
_____
_____
_____
_____
_____
_____
_____
_____
_____

Natasha D. Frazier

Week 18 - But with Power

"The Spirit of God, who raised Jesus from the dead, lives in you. And just as God raised Christ Jesus from the dead, he will give life to your mortal bodies by this same Spirit living within you." (Romans 8:11)

I have watched *The Lion King* movie at least 365 times. When my baby sister was about two years old, she wanted to watch it every day, and we did. Now that I am an adult with my own children, I have watched it a few times with them as well. *The Lion King* is a very powerful movie with several life lessons in it.

As a young cub, Simba was excited to become king. In fact, he sang about it and talked about it quite a bit. It was his destiny. He was born to become the next king and he knew this. As he grew older, Simba lost sight of who he was and who he was destined to be. He started to live as though he had no purpose because of something terrible that happened and discouraged him.

When Simba's newfound friends, Timon and Pumbaa, eventually learned that Simba was supposed to be king, their attitudes changed. Pumbaa started groveling at Simba's feet and Timon said, "Wait, he's not the king! Are you?" Simba then commented that he was going to be the king, but that was a long time ago. He reminded them that they didn't have to treat him differently because he was still the same person they knew. Timon said with a fist pump in the air, "Yes, but with *power*!" I love that part of the movie! It reminds me of us as God's children. When we accept Christ as our Savior, we receive the *power* of the Holy Spirit on the inside of us, becoming new creations. Don't take this lightly; you were created for purpose. Do not allow past circumstances to discourage you. If you have, it is time to reclaim the power that you have been given by the Holy Spirit and walk in the authority that you've been given.

Prayer: Heavenly Father, thank You for the power that You have given me through Your Holy Spirit. Help me not to lose sight of it and to always walk in Your strength and mighty power. In Jesus' name, Amen.

Further study: Romans 8

The Life Your Spirit Craves for Mommies

Week 18 - Journal

~

Have you ever allowed something in your past to hinder you from moving forward and live as though you have no purpose?

_____
_____
_____
_____
_____

Consider this: The same power that was at work in Jesus and raised Him from the dead, is also at work within us. God has promised us His Holy Spirit to comfort and guide us. What do you need to allow the Holy Spirit to work on in your life?

_____
_____
_____
_____
_____
_____

Commit to reclaim the power of the Holy Spirit and allow Him to work in your life. Write a prayer asking God to give you strength to allow His Holy Spirit to take control of the area in your life where you need to refocus and live according to the power of the Holy Spirit at work within you. God answers prayers and will grant your request to give you courage to walk in the mighty power that is already within you.

_____
_____
_____
_____
_____
_____

Natasha D. Frazier

Week 19 - Getting Dressed

"Therefore put on the full armor of God, so that when the day of evil comes, you may be able to stand your ground, and after you have done everything, to stand. Stand firm then, with the belt of truth buckled around your waist, with the breastplate of righteousness in place, and with your feet fitted with the readiness that comes from the gospel of peace. In addition to all this, take up the shield of faith, with which you can extinguish all the flaming arrows of the evil one. Take the helmet of salvation and the sword of the Spirit, which is the word of God." (Ephesians 6:13–17 NIV)

My daughter is absolutely obsessed by anything princess-related! Disney movies, dolls, and dresses. In fact, she associates any type of dress with being a princess. Whenever I wear a dress, she questions me as to whether I'm a queen or a princess. Whenever she wears a dress or a nightgown, she identifies herself as a princess and her attitude changes. She feels prettier and she acts differently, prancing around the house, twirling around in her dress. Even the phrase "getting dressed" is different to her. To her it means to *put on a dress* and not *put on clothes* as it does to the rest of us. See the obsession?

My question for you today is "what are you *wearing*?" Are you putting on the full armor of God? When you wear the full armor of God, is your attitude different? Do you feel strengthened? Are you more confident? You are an ambassador of Christ and what you "wear" should represent this fact. Take care not to neglect dressing your spirit man. What you're wearing spiritually is very important, as it will impact your attitude and your entire day. So take care to dress like God's royal child by putting on the full armor of God each day.

Prayer: Heavenly Father, thank You for the armor that You have provided for me. Let me not neglect *getting dressed* so that I may be able to stand firm in my faith. In Jesus' name, Amen.

Further study: Ephesians 6:10–20

The Life Your Spirit Craves for Mommies

Week 19 - Journal

~

Do you notice a difference in your day when you start it with God? Dressing your spirit with His Holy Word?

___

What keeps you from wearing the full armor of God every day?

___

Take the extra step this week, whether that means getting up early or adjusting your morning routine, and spend time each morning getting dressed in the spirit. Journal how this affects each day.

___

Natasha D. Frazier

Week 20 - No More Bubbles

"Blessed are those who find wisdom, those who gain understanding." (Proverbs 4:13 NIV)

My children are enthralled with bubbles. I recall once when I was taking a bubble bath, I couldn't get my daughter out of the bathroom. She was about two at the time. She soaked her clothes because she was busy reaching over into my tub full of bubbles, attempting to blow them into my face. We had a "bubble fight" and I blew bubbles toward her and they landed in her eyes. I wiped the bubbles off with a dry towel and we continued to play. Apparently she enjoyed it because she started rubbing bubbles into her own eyes (*on purpose*)! I, of course, insisted that she stop, but she would rub bubbles in her eyes and then say, "Ouch Mommy, it's itching." She continued to do this many times until I sent her out of the room to do something else.

Her shenanigans remind me of how we are with God. In this particular instance, I thought about how we as Christians continue to put *bubbles* in our eyes even when we know that it will cause some level of discomfort. We often know what the outcome will be when we do things like overeat (gluttony), procrastinate, lie, hold grudges, etc., but we continue to do them anyway. Why do we keep putting these *bubbles* in our eyes? Why do we continue to do things that will pull us away from God? Why do we not spend time reading our Bibles, studying, or praying?

Whatever your answers are to those questions, I pray that you recognize the bubbles for what they are: excuses and ploys of the enemy to keep you from growing in God. Things that will pop and fade, that will not last. As you go about your day, refuse to put *bubbles* in your eyes. Walk in wisdom and in the path that God has created for you.

Prayer: Heavenly Father, thank You for Your faithfulness. Help me to use knowledge and wisdom not to continue doing things that I know are damaging to myself and my relationship with You. In Jesus' name, Amen.

Further study: Proverbs 4

The Life Your Spirit Craves for Mommies

Week 20 - Journal

~

What bubbles do you continue to rub in your eyes even though you know it will cause some level of discomfort?

_____
_____
_____
_____
_____
_____
_____

Is this something that keeps you from growing in your relationship with God?

_____
_____
_____
_____
_____
_____
_____

If your bubbles keep you from growing in God, why do you allow them to interfere? Are you willing to trade this thing for your maturity in God? If so, this week, challenge yourself by replacing these bubbles with the Word of God. Each time you are tempted to play around with these bubbles, combat the temptation with prayer and/or the studying of God's word. Journal your progress this week.

_____
_____
_____
_____
_____
_____
_____

Natasha D. Frazier

Week 21 - Praise

"I will be filled with joy because of you. I will sing praises to your name, O Most High." (Psalm 9:2)

We were all in the car heading to church one morning when my husband glanced over at me, smiled, and said, "Hearing him sing a song with my name in it makes me feel really good."

You see our son, Ethan, who was a year old at the time, often made up songs with the words *Mommy* and *Daddy* in them. Of course the songs had other words, but who could make out what they were? They often went something like "Daddy, Daddy, Daddy" (repeat 20 times) or "Mommy, Mommy, Mommy" (repeat 20 times). It was so cute and it really did bring about a warm, refreshing feeling. That was one of his ways of showing affection for us as his parents.

When my husband made that comment to me, I couldn't help but wonder about how God must be pleased when we sing praises unto Him. The Bible reminds us over and over again, especially in the book of Psalms, to sing praises unto God. Have you had a song in your heart lately? How do you show your affection or love toward God?

Today, I encourage you to offer up a song of praise to God no matter how you're feeling. I can assure you that it will change your perspective in whatever you're dealing with and help shift your focus back to God. So go ahead, make God smile today!

Prayer: Heavenly Father, thank You for the gift of song. Even if I am musically challenged, please accept my praise as I lift You up in song today. Let my song be a reminder to me of who You are in my life, and a reflection of my love for You. In Jesus' name, Amen.

Further study: Psalm 150

The Life Your Spirit Craves for Mommies

Week 21 - Journal

~

In what ways do you show affection or love towards your Heavenly Father?

___

Have you had a song in your heart lately? What is it about that song that connects you with the Father?

___

Music is a gift and has a way of shifting our hearts and minds. If you haven't had a song in your heart recently, just praise God anyway! Lifting up praises to God often shifts our focus away from us and our problems to Him and His power. Even when you don't feel like it, sing anyway. This week, challenge yourself to sing praises to God when the cares of the world threaten to take over your mind. Journal the difference this makes.

___

Natasha D. Frazier

Week 22 - Always Hungry

"For he satisfies the thirsty and fills the hungry with good things." (Psalm 107:9)

As I was going through my daily task of cleaning the kitchen and sweeping the floor of the many crumbs and food pieces that seemed to find their way down, no matter what I cooked, I thought of how my children are *always* asking for snacks.

Before we leave the childcare center each day, they both grab a snack on the way out of the door. To keep down the fuss, I allow them to eat the snack in the car, even though I know their car seats will be filled with crumbs later.

By the time we make it home, they rush to the pantry to raid it for more snacks. Depending on how much longer it takes for dinner to be ready, I allow one more snack. I'm sure you know what's next, right? In a matter of minutes, they ask for another snack after scarfing down whatever they just ate.

I remember coming home from school feeling like I was going to starve. But I am amazed every single day that they don't seem to get enough–even after dinner, they want more snacks.

I found myself saying, "You guys are always hungry." But then I felt a nudge in my spirit saying, "What if you were always hungry for Me?" And I had to pause. How much better would my relationship with God be if I were always hungry for more of Him and fed that hunger with His Word, with prayer, with praise, or with worship?

Though my soul constantly thirsts for more of God, I don't always take time to get my fill of Him. What about you? Are you hungry and thirsty for the Lord? Are you getting your fill of Him? Today I encourage you to join me in feasting upon the Word of God and spending time in His presence. Our kids don't rest until their tummies are full. Why don't we seek sustenance for our spirit with that same eagerness?

Prayer: Heavenly Father, I want and need more of You. Today I'm choosing to replenish my soul by spending time meditating on Your Word and Your ways. In Jesus' name, thank You for always being willing to fill me, Amen.

Further study: Psalm 107

The Life Your Spirit Craves for Mommies

Week 22 - Journal

~

Do you take the time to fill your spirit with more of God when you're hungry or thirsty for more of Him? What prevents you from doing so?

_____
_____
_____
_____
_____

In what ways do you get your fill of God? As busy parents, it is imperative that we take time for ourselves and get more of Him. It may require waking up a few minutes earlier or staying awake a few minutes later, but it's well worth it in the end.

_____
_____
_____
_____
_____
_____
_____

Carve out a few extra minutes each day this week to spend time with God. If you already spend time with God in the mornings, challenge yourself to give a little more during some other time in your day. Refuel during lunch, a few minutes before picking up the kids or right before bed. Journal the impact this has on your day.

_____
_____
_____
_____
_____
_____
_____
_____

Natasha D. Frazier

Week 23 - Your Words Matter

"Wise words are more valuable than much gold and many rubies." (Proverbs 20:15)

Standing ten feet away from the microwave, my five-year-old would giggle and say that she couldn't see the time and needed to get closer to read it. Turns out that it wasn't a joke; she really did have trouble reading the time and seeing anything else that wasn't up close. Her pediatrician confirmed this at her well child check-up.

We received a referral to see an ophthalmologist. At that appointment, I was reminded of just how easily my words could have an effect on my child. A few seconds after the doctor began testing her, and she had already called a few wrong letters, the doctor and I began discussing some of the things I may have noticed at home. At that time, I brought up the microwave example. Those little ears were picking up everything because immediately, she began to repeat what I just said to the doctor, although she selected what she wanted to repeat. She repeated things such as, "It's too far away, so I can't see it." She didn't mention what I observed about her vision in other instances. Maybe she has selective hearing?

She stopped cooperating with the doctor; she only wanted to voice that she couldn't see. At that moment, I immediately realized how powerful and impactful my words are on her. I simply stated that she'd recently had trouble reading times on the microwave, but she took that to mean that she couldn't see and had given up on her eye test. Something about what I said made her believe that she couldn't see.

Have you spoken something to or around your child that has had an effect on them? Was it positive or negative? As parents, we have to realize that those little ears are always around listening and ready to soak up any information that they can receive, whether they should be listening or not, and whether or not we think they are paying attention. Today, let's choose to speak life, encouragement, and love into the soul and spirit of our children.

Prayer: Heavenly Father, thank You for the reminder of the impact that I have on my children. Help me to be mindful of what I say and do so that my ways and words may affect them positively and point them toward You. In Jesus' name, Amen.

Further study: Proverbs 18

The Life Your Spirit Craves for Mommies

Week 23 - Journal

~

Have you allowed what someone else has said about you to impact your life? Positive or negative? How so?

_____
_____
_____
_____
_____
_____
_____
_____
_____
_____

Have you noticed how your words impact the lives of your children? Positive or negative? How so?

_____
_____
_____
_____
_____
_____
_____
_____
_____
_____

Do you use your words to encourage or tear down others? Write about a time when you have done both and the impact your words had on your relationship with the other person?

_____
_____
_____

Write a prayer asking God to help you use your words to glorify Him, speak life and uplift others.

Be conscience of your words this week. Since you've written that prayer, you will likely be put in a situation where you have a clear choice to use your words for good. Journal about it.

The Life Your Spirit Craves for Mommies

Week 24 - A Moment Too Soon

"Wait patiently for the Lord. Be brave and courageous. Yes, wait patiently for the Lord." (Psalm 27:4)

We took our first family vacation to Disney World, where my mother, nephew, and youngest sister joined us. There aren't many roller coasters at Animal Kingdom, and of the few that were there, Expedition Everest was the largest. My sister, who was seventeen, walked hand in hand with my daughter right up to the entry gate for the ride. Now, I knew from reading the ride restrictions in the guide that my daughter wasn't tall enough to ride. Lagging behind the two of them, not really knowing where we were headed because my face was semi-glued to the map, I made it in enough time to see her walking away with tears in her eyes. "Mommy, he said I wasn't big enough to ride," she said in between sobs.

My heart was breaking for her because the trip was supposed to be fun and I had planned to keep her away from the rides I knew she wouldn't be able to ride. But because she went ahead of me, I wasn't able to protect her that one time. All I could do was promise that she would ride something the next day at Magic Kingdom, because I had already mapped out the things we would do at that particular park. Knowing that she would still be able to enjoy a roller coaster later made her feel better, gratefully.

That incident reminded me of how we are with God sometimes. We often move ahead of His plan for us, seeking our own gratification, only to later find out that we aren't ready for it. Or that one particular thing wasn't meant for us. We'd like to think that God will block things that aren't meant for us, but it doesn't always happen that way. I encourage you to choose God's will over your own. Join me in petitioning the throne of God before making decisions. When we seek His Word, we learn more of Him and His Will. Seeking God first will protect us from a lot of unnecessary hurts.

Prayer: Heavenly Father, I thank You for Your grace and mercy that are new each morning. I ask that You speak to my heart and lead me in my decision-making as I seek You first in all things. In Jesus' name, Amen.

Further study: 1 Corinthians 10:23; Psalm 37:4; Isaiah 40:31

Week 24 - Journal

~

Can you recall a time that you went ahead of God and the results were not as you'd hoped?

_____
_____
_____
_____
_____
_____
_____
_____

Can you recall a time when you prayed and waited for God's Holy nudging and the results were far greater than anything you could have imagined?

_____
_____
_____
_____
_____
_____
_____

Is there a prayer that you're currently waiting for God to answer? I encourage you to write it here and continue in faith and patience. When you receive your answer, return to this page and journal how God answered your prayer.

_____
_____
_____
_____
_____
_____
_____
_____

The Life Your Spirit Craves for Mommies

Week 25 - You Better Stop That

"Dear brothers and sisters, if another believer is overcome by some sin, you who are godly should gently and humbly help that person back onto the right path. And be careful not to fall into the same temptation yourself." (Galatians 6:1)

Sometimes it's hard to tell whether I'm the mother to my toddler or my daughter is. She fusses at him more than I do when he's up to no good. I suppose she's mirroring me? She does it often, but one day in particular, she was fussing at him for pouring water from his cup onto the high-chair tray. She screamed, "You better stop that!" Even though she acts like she's his parent, I chose to think positively about it and just deem her his accountability partner. If nothing else, she holds him accountable for everything he does and reminds him of the consequences of his actions at every chance she gets.

Although I don't always approve of how she tries to get her point across, I believe her intentions are good. I'd like to think that she's trying to keep him out of trouble, and she doesn't have a problem with telling him he's doing wrong. I wonder if we as Christians would be better off if we had an accountability partner in our face who didn't mind telling us when we were wrong. What if we had someone there to remind us of the consequences of our actions before we carry them out?

If you don't have an accountability partner, it is a great idea to get one to help you in your walk with being more like God. I encourage you to be bold and confident in the power of God and to encourage your brothers and sisters in their walk with God as well. We are here to love and lift one another up.

Prayer: Heavenly Father, thank You for Your Word and for those that You have placed in my life to help me and for me to help them. Let us be encouraged to know that You love us and that You desire for us to be more like You. Help us to remain faithful to Your Word and Your ways. In Jesus' name, Amen.

Further study: Proverbs 27:17; James 5:16; Ecclesiastes 4:9–12

Week 25 - Journal

~

Do you have someone in your life who you trust that will tell when you're wrong? Are you an accountability partner to someone else?

_____

Why do you think accountability partners are important?

_____

We've grown into a society that values privacy and quickly takes offense when someone points out our sin. How can we, as Christians, encourage our brothers and sisters who are caught up in sin to repent?

_____

The Life Your Spirit Craves for Mommies

Sometimes, our own sin keeps us from helping others come out of their sin. Think about your life. What can you do to change this if this is an issue for you? Write a prayer asking for God's guidance.

Natasha D. Frazier

Week 26 - Something Stinks

When Jesus heard this, he told them, 'Healthy people don't need a doctor—sick people do. I have come to call not those who think they are righteous, but those who know they are sinners.'" (Mark 2:17)

It's potty training time! If you've gone through this with any child already, you know how much of a struggle it is. Some days are good and others are not. However, I think the cheers are encouragement for our little guy.

One thing I've noticed throughout this process with him is that he tends to get really close to me when his training pants are dirty. Sometimes he tells me and other times not, but he makes sure that I smell him. He can be off playing with his sister for a long period, but when his training pants are dirty, he gets close to me. My guess is that he knows that I can clean up his mess. He knows where to turn when that situation gets messy and uncomfortable.

As God's children, we are the same way. Sometimes we put our relationship with God on the back burner, not spending as much time praying, studying our Bibles, or even practicing what the Word says, until we get into some mess. Once that happens, we find ourselves cuddling up next to God in prayer, spending more time reading our Bibles, going to church, etc. We do whatever it is we think we need to do to get cleansed.

We have the right idea—God is the only one who can free us from sin and clean up our mess. However, I'd like to encourage you to make time with God a priority, regardless of what's going on in your life. Don't just spend time with Him when you're stinky; spend time with Him when you're fresh too and perhaps you won't get stinky as much.

Prayer: Heavenly Father, thank You for Your forgiveness, grace, and mercy. Thank You for Your Son Jesus, who made the ultimate sacrifice so that we can be restored to You. Today, I ask that You continue to guide my heart toward You regardless of what state I'm in. I want my life to honor You at all times. In Jesus' name, Amen.

Further study: Luke 6:46–49

The Life Your Spirit Craves for Mommies

Week 26 - Journal

~

Have you ever put your relationship with God on the back burner, only to reconnect with Him when things aren't going well in your life?

What keeps you from making your relationship with God a priority?

Whether you currently consider yourself clean or stinky, take time this week to make your relationship with God a priority. It may require that you wake up earlier, stay up later or sacrifice time spent in some other area of your life. Write down your commitment here and journal your progress throughout this week. How has this impacted your week?

Natasha D. Frazier

Week 27 - Your Neighbor's Stuff

"You must not covet your neighbor's house. You must not covet your neighbor's wife, male or female servant, ox or donkey, or anything else that belongs to your neighbor." (Exodus 20:17)

Frozen. Most of us have watched that movie more times than we can count, or at least I have. My kids both love that movie and they both have character toys. My son had one plush Olaf, the snowman. When his second birthday came around, he received another one, but this one said phrases from the movie.

After we purchased the toy at Target and brought it home, my daughter picked up the regular plush toy and commented, "He already has Olaf; he doesn't need another one." Mind you, she has two Elsa dolls, one talking and one not, and I reminded her of that fact. However, she brings it up every time they play with the toys. Recently, I had to remind her not to count his toys and to worry about her own.

Aren't we like that sometimes? When people around us are blessed with some tangible item or a better position at work, or anything we deem they're unworthy of, we wonder why they have to get more, as if what they have isn't already enough.

Much like the lesson I'm trying to teach my daughter, we can learn from it as well: Do not covet your neighbor's things. (Part of the problem with my daughter is that she didn't get another toy for my son's birthday.) Whether we believe someone deserves something or not, we shouldn't be concerned or covet what they have. Everyone gets a turn; you just have to wait on yours.

Prayer: Heavenly Father, thank You for Your favor. I am reminded of Your goodness in my life. Help me to celebrate others when they receive tangible blessings, knowing that one day, I too will receive them. Thank You for Your kindness and for not being a respecter of persons. Because of this, I know and believe that I too can receive great things. In Jesus' name, Amen.

Further study: Psalm 119:36; Luke 12:15; Mark 7:21–23

The Life Your Spirit Craves for Mommies

Week 27 - Journal

~

Are you guilty of coveting something your neighbor has?

___

Do you ever feel like God is blessing everyone else but you? If so, why is this? Are you taking your eyes off God and focusing on those around you?

___

If you've had issues with jealousy and coveting, write a prayer asking God to change your heart and to remember who He is. The Word of God tells us in Psalm 24:1 that the earth is the Lord's and everything that dwells within it. If you believe that, be encouraged to know that God has all power to make anything happen in your life. If we spend time worrying about what God is doing in the life of the next person, we just might miss what he's trying to do in ours.

___

Natasha D. Frazier

Week 28 - You Hear What You Want to Hear

"My sheep listen to my voice; I know them, and they follow me." (John 10:27)

My toddler and kindergartener seem to have trouble from time to time hearing me call their names. Maybe it's because they know I'm about to ask them to do something they don't want to do. Turn off the television. Clean their rooms. Pick up their toys. Get ready for a bath. Get ready for naptime or bedtime.

However, I never have problems getting their attention when it comes to snacks. The same deaf ear that needed to hear their names twenty times just ten minutes before doesn't even require a call when they hear the pantry door opening. The rattling of a bag of potato chips or the rumbling of a bag of goldfish crackers always seems to grab their attention instantly, without me saying a word. Sometimes it's almost as if they can sense that I'm near the pantry and they make a beeline to my side making snack requests.

I laugh at this, but it reminds me of us as children of God. When it comes to the voice of God leading us to do things that we're uncomfortable with, we're hesitant. That hesitant spirit will often dissipate if the calling was for something we've been praying for or something we deem we need from God. My mom often said, "You hear what you want to hear," when I didn't do what she asked of me.

I encourage you to join me in committing to moving with the same haste to the voice of God regardless of what He is asking of us. Let's choose to be obedient and willing to follow the Word and ways of God.

Prayer: Heavenly Father, I often fall short when it comes to being obedient to Your voice. I ask that You give me a willing heart to follow You in everything, whether I am uncomfortable or content. I want to be all that You desire of me. In Jesus' name, Amen.

Further study: John 10

The Life Your Spirit Craves for Mommies

Week 28 - Journal

~

Is there something that the Holy Spirit has been nudging you to do but you're hesitant? If so, why?

_____
_____
_____
_____
_____
_____
_____
_____

Is there a difference in your response to God's Holy Spirit when it's an answered prayer vs. something that you're uncomfortable with?

_____
_____
_____
_____
_____
_____
_____
_____

If it is your desire, write a prayer asking God to give you courage and an obedient and willing spirit, to listen to and follow His voice.

_____
_____
_____
_____
_____
_____
_____
_____

Natasha D. Frazier

Week 29 - Detours Are Necessary

"This is my command—be strong and courageous! Do not be afraid or discouraged. For the Lord your God is with you wherever you go." (Joshua 1:9)

Houston morning and evening traffic is often a mess: accidents, snail paced, and frustrating. In the event of rain or any other type of inclement weather, the traffic becomes one hundred times worse. One morning while shuffling my kids off to school, it was rainy and traffic was pretty bad. Traffic is hardly ever backed up to the exit we use to enter the nearest highway, but this morning, it was. Add to that, a train had paused on the railroad tracks (we needed to cross the tracks on our normal route to get to the school), and it looked like our ten-minute drive was about to turn into a thirty-minute drive. Luckily for us, I hadn't passed up the street that would allow us to make a detour around the train.

Of course, my little backseat driver fussed the entire time telling me that I was going the wrong way. She constantly asked where I was going and why I was going in that direction. It amazes me how well she knows directions! Anyway, I kept reassuring her that it was necessary that we take a new route and that we would still get to the school. "There is more than one way to get there," I told her.

Many times, life will throw a few curveballs our way that will make us need to take a detour in order to get to where we're going. Financial setbacks, health issues, job issues, family crisis—no matter what the issue is, and no matter how far it may seem you are from your destination, rest assured that God has promised to never leave you and to be your guide. You will get to where you need to be in life, even if you're not taking the shortest route or the route you thought you would be taking. A different route may even be best to help you avoid collision.

Prayer: Heavenly Father, thank You for Your Word that is my life's navigation. Whether I fall off course by my own doing or life's circumstances, I am thankful that You are still there and You promised to never leave me or forsake me. Your Word says that You will be with me wherever I may go. Thank You for Your love and grace. In Jesus' name, Amen.

Further study: John 14:15–17

The Life Your Spirit Craves for Mommies

Week 29 - Journal

~

Recall a time when you had to take a detour in life. At the time, could you see that it was necessary? Now that the event has passed, can you see why it was necessary? Did knowing that God was with you give you the courage to get through it? Why or why not?

_____
_____
_____
_____
_____
_____
_____
_____
_____
_____

There are times when an alternate route is absolutely necessary. Whether you're experiencing it now or not, at some point you will. Write a prayer asking God to give you strength and courage to get through that time. Detours are not always easy to accept but God's word is a lamp unto our feet and a light unto our path. We need Him to get through it.

_____
_____
_____
_____
_____
_____
_____
_____
_____

Natasha D. Frazier

Week 30 - Preparing Before You Go

"Trust in the Lord with all your heart; do not depend on your own understanding. Seek his will in all you do, and he will show you which path to take."(Proverbs 3:5–6)

Have you ever watched *Mickey Mouse Clubhouse*? I may have watched more of those shows than I'd like to admit. Both of my children love the show and characters. One thing amazes me about the show, however. Before Mickey and his friends set out on any adventure, they call Toodles (Mickey's helper) so that he can show them their Mouseketools (items that will help them somewhere in their journey for that day). There are usually about four items, with one being a mystery item. Along their journey, when they are faced with an issue, they call Toodles and he appears with their Mouseketools. Mickey and his friends go through the process of elimination in choosing which tool would be the most likely to help them solve the problem. They select the tool and Toodles goes away.

Now I'm not sure if there's something I'm missing, but I've always wondered *how* does Toodles even *know* what to bring in the first place? How does he know what Mickey and his friends are going to be faced with that day? I still don't have the answer to those questions, and I've watched that show for years, but it made me think about us as Christians.

We don't know what we will be faced with each day, but God has given us a way to prepare for it: studying His Word and seeking Him in prayer. I think those are very useful tools to aid us in getting our day started, before we leave home, start work, and take on the day. I encourage you to use the tools that are available to you to prepare for your day. As a mom, I know how tough and unpredictable mornings can be, but waking up a little early and using those extra minutes as time alone with God is precious and can have a huge impact on my day. You don't have to call Toodles, but you do have the privilege of calling upon the Holy Spirit. Try it today.

Prayer: Heavenly Father, thank You for the opportunity to come before Your throne at any time. Thank You that my time alone with You refreshes, renews, and prepares me for my day. Thank You for the power of Your Word. In Jesus' name, Amen.

Further study: Proverbs 4:10–12

The Life Your Spirit Craves for Mommies

Week 30 - Journal

~

What steps do you usually take to prepare for your day?

_____
_____
_____
_____
_____
_____
_____
_____

What is one thing you can work on to help you better prepare for the day ahead? Work on that thing this week and journal how it impacts your day each day.

_____
_____
_____
_____
_____
_____
_____
_____
_____
_____
_____
_____

Write a prayer asking God to go before you and make your paths straight. God has the privilege of seeing things that we cannot see. Lean on His still small voice to guide you.

_____
_____
_____
_____
_____
_____

Natasha D. Frazier

Week 31 - Special Assignments

"There are different kinds of spiritual gifts, but the same Spirit is the source of them all." (1 Corinthians 12:4)

Paw Patrol is a cartoon show about puppies that have special skills to solve problems, such as that of a construction worker, firefighter, etc. We watched two shows back-to-back. In the first show, each of the puppies got a chance to use its special skill to help a human friend, all in one scene. In the second show, only a few puppies were called to help and the others would jump in whenever their special skill was needed; otherwise they would work in the background to accomplish the task. To my five-year-old, it didn't make sense. She asked me why one puppy (girl puppy wearing pink who could fly an airplane—her favorite after one show) didn't get an assignment. I tried to explain that she was still useful even though she didn't have a special assignment. Amidst my explanation, they needed said puppy's help. That helped solidify my point that although her skills weren't needed when the rescue task initially started, that didn't mean that she wasn't important and that they weren't going to need her at all. She just had to take a backseat in the beginning.

Now the puppy wasn't bothered by it, because she knew her place. Oftentimes, we as Christians get bent out of shape when we're not in front or haven't been called on to lead. We have to be careful to operate in our gifts and in God's timing. Just because it's not your turn now, doesn't mean you won't get a turn.

So if you've ever had issues with thinking you aren't useful because you're not called to lead, then I encourage you to think again. Reading your Bible, you will find many people who did great things who weren't necessarily in the forefront. Everyone has a place. Remember that you are needed where you are and can be useful right where you are planted.

Prayer: Heavenly Father, thank You for the wisdom to know that You have me where You need me to be and that I can be assured that I am most effective where You have me planted. Let me not have a heart of envy or jealously toward my sister or brother. In Jesus' name, Amen.

Further study: 1 Corinthians 12

The Life Your Spirit Craves for Mommies

Week 31 - Journal

~

Do you have issues with working behind-the-scenes? Why or why not?

_____
_____
_____
_____
_____
_____

Do you believe that God has called you to do something greater and those in higher positions do not recognize your worth or your calling? Do you ever feel like you're being held back? Read Ecclesiastes 3:1-16.

_____
_____
_____
_____

When is it going to be my time? A question we often ask ourselves. Sometimes we move too quickly and other times we procrastinate. Timing is a very sensitive issue and we have to get to a place where we're hearing from God and being obedient. Seasons change and we need to be ready for the time when God wants to use us in a different way. Write a prayer asking God to give you an open heart and mind that is willing to obey His Holy promptings.

_____
_____
_____
_____
_____
_____

Natasha D. Frazier

Week 32 - Will You Pray for Me?

"Don't worry about anything; instead, pray about everything. Tell God what you need, and thank him for all he has done." (Philippians 4:6)

Both of my children were piled onto my lap while watching cartoons one Friday night. My daughter was the second to claim her spot. As she made herself comfortable, she told me that she would only be there until her eye stopped hurting. But then she looked up at me and asked, "Mommy, will you pray for me?" Proud mommy moment. That warmed my heart and convicted me.

Usually when someone requests that I pray for them, I pray at a later time. But not for my baby. How could I wait? She had enough faith to believe that God could stop her eye from hurting, and that all we needed to do was pray about it. *Ask and it shall be given unto you.* So we prayed right then, asking God to heal her eye and remove any pain; agreeing, each child echoed "Amen" at the close of the prayer.

As adults, a red and itchy eye may not seem like something *big* enough to pray to God about. But to my daughter (and other small children and new believers) it was enough. Not too big or too small. She just had the knowledge of where to take her problem and believe that it would be done.

So tonight I took a note from her. I've had way more Bible study and time with God than she has and still I am often picky about what I should pray about. Maybe it's because I think that some people have far greater issues or the issue is something that doesn't really *require* prayer. But no more. I will exercise my faith as that of a child and pray about everything, as God's Word instructs. There is no caveat about anything being too small; the idea is that God wants a relationship with us, and relationships are forged through communication. Prayer. I encourage you to join me in seeking God with the spirit of a child: humble and full of faith.

Prayer: Heavenly Father, thank You for Your Word and for getting the point across through children. Your Word is true and never changing, and today I submit to Your Word and choose to pray about everything. I believe that You hear me and have faith that You will answer. In Jesus' name, Amen.

Further study: Philippians 4:6–9

The Life Your Spirit Craves for Mommies

Week 32 - Journal

~

Have you ever not prayed about something because you thought it was insignificant?

_____
_____
_____
_____
_____
_____
_____

What prevents you from praying about everything?

_____
_____
_____
_____
_____
_____
_____

This week, pray about everything. Whenever something bothers you, pray about it. Thinking about how much God loves you, thank Him in prayer. Worried about something, stop and pray. Someone asks you to pray, stop and pray in that moment. Kids driving you insane, pray about it. No matter how big or small the issue may be, pray about it. You won't have enough space to write down everything, but each day, write down the highlights and how praying about everything impacted your day.

_____
_____
_____
_____
_____
_____
_____

Natasha D. Frazier

Week 33 - Apple of My Eye

"Be still, and know that I am God! I will be honored by every nation. I will be honored throughout the world." (Psalm 46:10)

One day my son asked for an apple. He only wanted it because he saw his sister with one, or so I thought. I usually wash, peel, and chop up her apple before giving it to her, and so I did the same thing for him. Now, I believed I was doing what was best for him (cutting up the apple so that he wouldn't choke), but he did not like it. He had a fit! He started crying and pointing. He was becoming hysterical for seemingly no reason at all. Turns out that he wanted to bite the apple himself. He didn't want an apple that was already cut up.

Cutting up the apple was the best thing for him at the time. That was my way of ensuring that he didn't bite off too much or choke on the apple peel. But for him, that was the worst thing ever. He couldn't see that I was trying to protect him and help him out a little. All he saw is that I was ruining his apple.

Have you ever received something and then it seemed like God was taking it away from you? Or things weren't going your way? Started a new job only to get laid off? A relationship that seemed as if it was going great but all of a sudden the communication stopped? At the time anything like this happened, you might have thought that God was making some sort of mistake and your blessing was being ripped to pieces. In hindsight, you can probably look back on it and see that God was making things better for you. He can see far ahead of where you are right now and knows how to protect you.

Oftentimes, in the midst of unlikely situations, we can't see that. But just like my son had to learn (and is still learning) that I know what's best, we have to learn that same thing about God. He knows what's best and His love for us is far greater than anything that we can fathom.

Prayer: Heavenly Father, help me to trust in You and believe that You know all things and have my best interest in mind. Thank You for Your love. In Jesus' name, Amen.

Further study: Psalm 46

The Life Your Spirit Craves for Mommies

Week 33 - Journal

~

Can you recall a time when God allowed something great to happen in your life only for it to be taken away a short while later? Did you find yourself questioning God as to why it happened? Can you now see the good in it?

_____
_____
_____
_____
_____

Is there something that God has allowed to happen that you still can't see how it was good for you? Write it here and then copy today's scripture. Even though we don't always understand or receive the answers we seek, we have to know that God is God and His thoughts are greater than our thoughts and His ways are greater than our ways.

_____
_____
_____
_____
_____
_____
_____
_____

Write a prayer thanking God for being all knowing and all powerful. Ask that He gives you strength to trust in Him and hold tight to His Word in times when you don't understand or can't see how He's working on your behalf.

_____
_____
_____
_____
_____

Natasha D. Frazier

Week 34 - Even Though it's Good for Me

Whatever is good and perfect is a gift coming down to us from God our Father, who created all the lights in the heavens. He never changes or casts a shifting shadow." (James 1:7)

We were preparing to leave out the door for school on a Monday morning and I was doing a backpack check. When I lifted my daughter's backpack, I noticed that it was heavy, far heavier than it should have been for the one folder that was supposed to be in it. When I opened it, her lunch bag was still inside with an apple that she was supposed to have eaten Friday with the rest of her lunch.

When I pointed it out to her, she said, "Yea, Momma, I know the apple is in there, but I didn't want it." She continued, "I know apples are good for me, but I didn't want an apple, so I didn't eat it."

We as adults can be like that every single day. We know that spending time in prayer is good for us, but we skip it or breeze through it. We know that studying God's Word is good for us, but we put it off until later. We know that exercising is good for us, but we'll get to it next week. And the list goes on.

What is it that you know is good for you—but you neglect to do it? Today I encourage you to embrace those things that are good for you, whether or not you like doing them or whether or not you think you have time for them. There is no better time to invest in your spiritual growth. Your children need you to be the best *you* that you can be.

Prayer: Heavenly Father, thank You for reminding me that I neglect many things that are good for me, including spending quality time with You. Help me to set aside those things that aren't worthwhile and to make time for those things that are. Thank You for Your grace and mercy that are new to me each day. Help me to become the woman and mother that you have created me to be. In Jesus' name, Amen.

Further study: Matthew 6:33

The Life Your Spirit Craves for Mommies

Week 34 - Journal

~

What are some habits that you've formed that aren't good for you but yet you continue to do them anyway?

___

What are some things that are good for you that you put them off to do at a later time?

___

When it comes to your relationship with God and spending time with Him, do you put it off for a later time? Why?

___

Choose two things this week that are good for you (and you've been putting off) and be intentional about doing those things this week. Try replacing the things that aren't good for you for the things that are. Journal about your experience each day.

The Life Your Spirit Craves for Mommies

Week 35 - I'm Sorry

"Even if that person wrongs you seven times a day and each time turns again and asks forgiveness, you must forgive." (Luke 17:4)

Every now and again when my children get into an argument and things get out of control, perhaps the toddler hits the older one or takes something and runs, I have to restore order. This usually ends with me instructing him to apologize to his sister. I step away and allow them the space they need to make up.

My son walks toward his sister with his arms outstretched apologizing. Two simple words—"I'm sorry"—end all troubles for the moment. She accepts his hug and apology and then tells him that it's all right. After hugging it out, they resume playing. I'm always amazed that she can let it go or, vice versa, instantly. There are no grudges or reminders about what recently happened. Only love and forgiveness.

I often ask myself, "Is that really all it takes?" Surely something else has to be done but for them, that's it. I know that many things happen to us over time that a simple apology may not be able to fix, but I have learned a lot from watching the two of them in times like this.

Love and forgiveness help us to move on with our lives. God's Word even instructs us to forgive so that we may be forgiven. When we are wronged, we often forget that we ourselves have also been on the other side hurting others. I encourage you to examine your life. If you are harboring any unforgiveness, let it go. Remember that forgiveness is not only for the one who wronged you but for you too; it frees you and allows you to move forward.

Prayer: Heavenly Father, thank You for the power of forgiveness. Forgive me as I forgive those who have wronged me. Let me not be one who holds on to grudges or have a hardened heart. I want to be one who loves others in a way that pleases You. In Jesus' name, Amen.

Further study: Luke 17:3–5

Week 35 -Journal

~

What has happened in your life that keeps you from moving forward? Why can't you forgive and move on?

Does knowing that God's Word commands us to forgive have an impact on your willingness to forgive? Does the fact that you, too, have to daily ask God for forgiveness have an impact on your willingness to forgive? Why or why not?

If you are harboring any unforgiveness in your heart, I challenge you to first write a prayer asking God to help you truly move on. Then, as hard as it may be, forgive.

The Life Your Spirit Craves for Mommies

Forgive so that you can move forward and allow God to replace that hurt with love and mercy.

_____
_____
_____
_____
_____
_____
_____
_____
_____
_____

Natasha D. Frazier

Week 36 - I Can Do It Myself

"Two people are better off than one, for they can help each other succeed." (Ecclesiastes 4:9)

"I don't need your help, Mommy; I can do it by myself," says my daughter when she's trying to learn something new or prove that she is *big enough* do something without me. The latest of these statements came when she was learning to tie her shoes. Although I encourage independence, I rarely want to hear about this independence when we're on our way out of the door in the morning and we should have left fifteen minutes before.

Most of the time, she is right—she doesn't need my help. But then there are times when she and I both know that she needs my help doing something, and yet she refuses it. She will try and try until she becomes frustrated, and then she yells out to me to rescue her. I often have to remind her that it's okay to need help, and that she doesn't have to do everything on her own because I'm here.

That can be us too. No prayer. No studying God's Word. Just ready, set, take off. When we don't take advantage of the spiritual tools that are available to us, it's as if we're telling God the same thing: *I don't need You right now, Lord; I can do it by myself.* God also has placed people in our lives to help us along the way, yet we often refuse help and attempt to accomplish things on our own when we don't have to.

Undoubtedly there are decisions that shouldn't be made without spending time in prayer and study first; and journeys that shouldn't be embarked upon alone. God's Word reminds us that two are better than one. So I encourage you to first connect with God before doing anything, and then receive the help that God will give to you through others along the way.

Prayer: Heavenly Father, thank You for the promises in Your Word that You will never leave me nor forsake me. I thank You that Your Word is a lamp unto my feet and a light unto my path. Thank You for those You have put in my path to help me in my journey so that I don't have to go through it alone. In Jesus' name, Amen.

Further study: Ecclesiastes 4:9–12

The Life Your Spirit Craves for Mommies

Week 36 - Journal

~

When is the last time your actions said, *I can do it myself?* What was the result?

_____
_____
_____
_____
_____
_____
_____
_____
_____
_____

Do you have issues asking or accepting help from others? Why or why not? Do you recognize when God has placed a particular person in your path to help you?

_____
_____
_____
_____
_____
_____
_____
_____
_____
_____

Are you carefully considering God's Word and seeking Him through prayer before making decisions? What keeps you from praying and waiting for God to answer?

_____
_____
_____
_____

Natasha D. Frazier

Week 37 - He Helps Me Up

"The faithful love of the Lord never ends! His mercies never cease. Great is his faithfulness; his mercies begin afresh each morning." (Lamentations 3:22–23)

I do morning drop-offs—taking the kids to school and daycare. Typically the kids and I leave before my husband does. He sees us off by giving hugs and kisses, making sure that we're all buckled in, praying, and then returning inside the house so that he can finish his morning preparations before leaving for work.

Most mornings after this routine, my daughter comments that she's going to miss her daddy and cannot wait until we all get home in the evening. One morning, she went on about how she was going to miss him and that she loves him. It was the reason *why* she said she loved him that gave me pause. "Mommy, I love Daddy because he helps me up when I fall." There are several truths in her statement. She understands that her daddy loves her because he helps her. And the second truth is that the Lord loves us enough to help us too, but in a much greater way than earthly fathers.

The Lord is always there for us when we're hurting, when we fall, or when we're in a sphere of doubt about what's to come. No matter the circumstances, He is always there. When we're in sin, He's there, and because of His mercy we are not consumed. His compassion includes protection from the wrath that we should receive but don't.

Contemplate some of the reasons that you love God and ways that He has demonstrated that He loves you. One thing is for sure, God is faithful, loving, and merciful to us. His love is everlasting; it endures forever. Grasp onto the love of God today. Stand firm in His love and His commitment to you. Remember that He is always there when you need Him, even when you perceive you do not.

Prayer: Heavenly Father, thank You for the sweet reminders that Your love endures forever and that You are always near. I give You praise for the joy that You've placed in my heart. Help me to hold fast to the fact that You are forever present and that Your love never fades. In Jesus' name, Amen.

Further study: Psalm 118

The Life Your Spirit Craves for Mommies

Week 37 - Journal

~

What are some of the reasons why you love God? In what ways has He shown that He loves you?

_____
_____
_____
_____
_____
_____
_____
_____

As Lamentations 3:22-23 reminds us, God's love endures forever and his mercies never end. Be reminded of that this week. Write a prayer thanking God for His unending love, mercy and faithfulness.

_____
_____
_____
_____
_____
_____
_____
_____
_____
_____

The Holy Spirit is our helper. He is always there. What do you need to lean on your helper for this week?

_____
_____

Natasha D. Frazier

Week 38 - Winners Do Not Give Up

"I don't mean to say that I have already achieved these things or that I have already reached perfection. But I press on to possess that perfection for which Christ Jesus first possessed me." (Philippians 3:12)

We were riding to school one morning when what seemed like out of nowhere, my daughter said, "Momma, winners don't quit. Winners don't give up. Right, Momma?" I agreed with her but had no clue what triggered the thought. Eventually she told me that another child in her class was upset one day and blurted out, "I give up!"

She then went into this line of questioning about giving up and why we shouldn't give up. As you can see, she keeps me on my toes. I had already started the DVD player for her and her brother, thinking that it would be a mostly quiet ride and I could drink my coffee while doing my own meditation. She quickly changed that for me and gave me something more to think about.

The key point is that *winners* don't give up. If you give up, you can't win. Sure, life can get tough with careers, ministry, children, family, businesses, and trying to pursue your dreams, but that is no reason to give up. You may at times have to shift your focus or take a break, but you shouldn't give up.

I'm not sure where my daughter even heard that phrase, but she's on the right track. Whatever you're up to, God placed it on your heart for a reason. If you need to take a step back and assess what you're doing, do so, but don't quit. Depend on the Holy Spirit to guide you along the way.

Prayer: Heavenly Father, thank You for the strength that You provide to me through Your Holy Spirit. Help me to stand firm when times get hard and to remember that my work is committed to You. Thank You for Your wisdom and direction. In Jesus' name, Amen.

Further study: Philippians 3:12–13; Colossians 3:23

The Life Your Spirit Craves for Mommies

Week 38 - Journal

~

Have you been so overwhelmed that you have considered giving up? Why? I find that most times when I become overwhelmed, it is because I'm thinking about every single thing that I have to do. When you focus on things this way, it's easier to want to quit. God didn't create the world in one day, so surely He doesn't expect you to finish everything at once. Little by little, you shall accomplish your goals.

_____
_____
_____
_____
_____

What keeps you motivated?

_____
_____
_____
_____
_____

If there's something you're working on right now that seems too big for you to handle, write down everything you think needs to be done and create a checklist. Pray over that list and ask God to give you wisdom, direction and help to accomplish that goal. Doing a little at a time will get you where you need to be. Scratching items off that list will encourage you, too. *Winners* don't give up.

_____
_____
_____
_____
_____

Week 39 - More, Please

"The master was full of praise. 'Well done, my good and faithful servant. You have been faithful in handling this small amount, so now I will give you many more responsibilities. Let's celebrate together!'" (Matthew 25:21)

One night after dinner, I was standing over the kitchen sink, nearly elbow deep in dishwater, when my toddler made a special request. "Momma, I want more. More chicken." He smiled as he finished off the last piece of meat in his hands. It's in these times that I often feel a sense of accomplishment for a few minutes. Why? Like most toddlers, mine is often very picky about his food and tonight dinner was a success. He liked it and he wanted seconds. In fact, both kids were relatively quiet during dinner, not the usual playing, chattering, and endless requests to leave the table.

The whole scene may seem miniscule, but not to me. See, I'm usually pretty strategic when it comes to leftovers during the week, but this was a Friday evening. Not having leftovers doesn't bother me on the weekends, because I have more time to cook, unlike the weekdays. So when he asked, I had more to give him. Clearing his plate meant he had room for more and he knew exactly how to get it. Ask.

As God's children, we go to Him when we are in need—when we need to be filled. Ethan's request sent my mind along a trail of thoughts that paused with this: How much more does our Heavenly Father have in store for us if we would just clear our plates? Our life's plate is often filled with so many things that get in the way or distract us from what God really wants to give us—more of Him. So many times we ask God for more of something when we haven't done anything with what we already have. One could ask for more, but the question we should ask ourselves is, "Is there room for it?" Is it time to clear your plate?

Prayer: Heavenly Father, thank You for the reminder that You are ever present, willing, and able to give me what I need. Examine my heart and help me to be a good steward over the time and resources you've given me. Help me to know when it's time to clear my plate so that I can receive more of You. In Jesus' name, Amen.

Further study: Matthew 25:14–30

The Life Your Spirit Craves for Mommies

Week 39 - Journal

~

Have you been asking God for more of something when you haven't done anything with what He's already given you?

_____
_____

What do you need God to grant you more of today? What are you willing to give up in exchange?

_____
_____
_____
_____
_____
_____
_____

Take a moment to examine your life. Are there things on your plate that you need to remove in order to spend more time with God? Are there some activities that you need to say "no" to in order to achieve balance? Are you doing something that doesn't add value to your life?

_____
_____
_____
_____
_____

If you find during your examination that there are things you need to let go of, start making that change today. God probably won't add anything to you if you don't have room for it.

_____
_____
_____
_____
_____

Natasha D. Frazier

Week 40 - The Things You Can Control

"And now, dear brothers and sisters, one final thing. Fix your thoughts on what is true, and honorable, and right, and pure, and lovely, and admirable. Think about things that are excellent and worthy of praise." (Philippians 4:8)

Bedtime for my toddler used to be so easy. All I had to do was stick to our bedtime routine: bath, stories, and prayer. Afterwards, he'd be reaching for the bed. My daughter was the one who refused to sleep and had every excuse under the sun as to why she needed to get out of bed. (This situation has now been reversed.)

I often told her to keep her noise to a minimum while she went through whatever she needed to do to get to sleep. The last thing I wanted was for both of them to have trouble getting to and staying asleep. Once after this conversation, she asked, "Well, what about the cars outside? What about the dogs barking?" I explained that we cannot control the noise outside of the house, but we can control the noise that we make inside the house, and that is what we should focus on.

So often, we focus on all of the things that we cannot control: other people, outside influences, and all sorts of external things. When we concentrate on stuff we cannot do anything about, we neglect to do something about the stuff we can, and then we find chaos all around us.

We must focus on our thoughts, our decisions, and our actions. *Am I bringing honor to God by thinking, saying, or doing this? Am I overly concerned about things I can't do anything about?*

May your thoughts and actions bring honor to God as you choose to please Him.

Prayer: Heavenly Father, thank You for Your Word that encourages me to think about those things that honor You. Help me not to be concerned with what is beyond my control but to embrace what I have dominion over and bring honor to You. In Jesus' name, Amen.

Further study: Philippians 4:8–9; Isaiah 26:3; Psalm 104:34

The Life Your Spirit Craves for Mommies

Week 40 - Journal

~

Do you find yourself overly concerned about things that you cannot change? Why?

_____
_____
_____
_____
_____
_____
_____
_____
_____
_____

How do you deal with things that are beyond your control? Do you allow them to cause worry?

_____
_____
_____
_____
_____
_____
_____
_____
_____
_____

Our thoughts manifest into actions, good or bad. What are some things you do to control your thoughts? When your thoughts spiral down a path that is not pleasing to God, how do you bring yourself back to a place where your thoughts are worthy of praise?

When we focus on the wrong things, life can get out of control, sometimes quicker than we realize. Write a prayer asking God to help you control your thoughts and give you a heart and mind sensitive to His voice. Don't give the enemy room in your mind. What can you do to combat thoughts that aren't pleasing to God? Practice doing this on a daily basis.

The Life Your Spirit Craves for Mommies

Week 41 - A Day Off

"'My thoughts are nothing like your thoughts,' says the Lord. 'And my ways are far beyond anything you could imagine.'" (Isaiah 55:8)

I get excited about holidays that give me time off work. In fact, there are about three holidays where I'm off work and my children still have to go to school. I'm always looking forward to these days, never really having any definite plans, but eagerly waiting for them nonetheless.

President's Day was coming. I had been very tired, so I planned to catch up on rest. In fact, I'd been saying, "Lord, I just need a day off." I guess I should have been specific because I got sick. I thought I would still be able to get some rest but not so. My baby was sick on my sick day. A couple of weeks later, President's Day arrived, but I didn't get to enjoy it as planned. You see, my son, who was about eighteen months old at the time, decided that he would jump out of his crib. Because of that, I spent my holiday at the doctor's office.

Although I had been looking forward to time off alone, I chose to look at it from a different light. Both of those incidents gave me more precious time with him. With two children, very seldom do I have the opportunity to spend time with one without the other, but this time I did. I'd like to think he enjoyed the individual attention as well.

So even when things don't go your way, find a way to see the good in the situation. And not only to see the good but to see God. He is always working on our behalf. Things can always be worse than what they are, so rejoice and be thankful for God's love, grace, and mercy.

Prayer: Heavenly Father, thank You for allowing me to see You in every situation. Help me to keep my heart and mind focused on You and to rejoice in Your love for me. Even when I'm not in control, You always are. I find comfort in that. In Jesus' name, Amen.

Further study: 1 Timothy 6:6; Isaiah 55:8–9

Week 41 - Journal

~

Think about a time when something didn't go your way. Did you get upset? How did you handle it? Can you think of anything positive that came out of that situation?

_____
_____
_____
_____
_____
_____
_____
_____
_____
_____

Many times we don't see things the way God sees them. Can you recall a recent situation wherein the natural realm things didn't seem to go well, but from a spiritual perspective, it did?

_____
_____
_____
_____
_____
_____
_____
_____
_____

As you go about your week, choose to think of every situation the way you think God would see it. Shining God's love, grace, and mercy on a situation is sure to give you a different perspective. Journal about the impact this has on your life this week.

The Life Your Spirit Craves for Mommies

Week 42 - The Helper

"But when the Father sends the Advocate as my representative—that is, the Holy Spirit—he will teach you everything and will remind you of everything I have told you." (John 14:26)

My daughter is such a great helper. In fact, she prides herself on being Mommy's helper and makes sure to remind me of such from time to time. I often let her assist with things I know she can handle, such as helping to put dishes away, folding towels, or going to find something in the house for me. She helps me with her little brother too—grabbing training pants, helping him find his cup or shoes. One morning, I saw her trying to help him into his training pants! Sometimes, I have to admit, it's cute and it warms my heart. But other times, she is so helpful or insists on helping so much that I wonder if I really *need* the help. Like, do I look like I'm struggling or something? Or is it just her innate ability? Her teacher has mentioned that she is quite the leader, so maybe it's a little bit of both. The most interesting thing is that although she insists she's my helper, she really only wants to help when it's convenient for her.

In the spiritual realm, the Holy Spirit was sent by Jesus Himself to help us. The Holy Spirit is ever present and we don't have to worry about Him being tired and only assisting when He feels like it or when it's convenient. The Holy Spirit provides comfort and guidance to us. He is often that small voice that says "don't do this" or "go this way."

I encourage you to open your heart to God's Holy Spirit today and allow Him to guide you and show you God's way in every area of your life. We sometimes get so busy that we forget that the help that God has sent is only a breath away.

Prayer: Thank You for Your Holy Spirit that You have sent to be with me wherever I may go. Thank You for loving me enough to not leave me alone in this world but to provide Your Holy Spirit, who is everything that I need. In Jesus' name, Amen.

Further study: John 14:15–31

The Life Your Spirit Craves for Mommies

Week 42 - Journal

~

Have you ever said, "Something told me to do that!" Most of us are guilty of using that phrase. That Something is Someone - the Holy Spirit. Do you find yourself taking that course of action that the Holy Spirit, that small voice, advises you to take?

_____
_____
_____
_____

There are times when we don't recognize that it was God speaking to us until after the fact. Do you agree? Why do you think this is so?

_____
_____
_____
_____
_____

Write a prayer asking God to assist you with being sensitive to His voice. Sometimes we're in such a rush that we miss it, but this week, listen intently for that small voice and do what It says. Journal how this changes the course of your day.

_____
_____
_____
_____
_____
_____
_____

Natasha D. Frazier

Week 43 - Because of Who You Are

"I will praise the Lord at all times. I will constantly speak his praises." (Psalm 34:1)

When I pick my children up from school each day, they seem so excited to see me. Most days they run, full-force, straight to me, throw their little arms around my neck, and tell me how much they miss me and love me. But soon after, there is a request for something: snacks, juice, TV, Disney World, Chuck E. Cheese's, going outside, etc. You name it, it's on their list.

On the other hand, some days I am shown all this love but there is no request at all. It feels good to be loved just because of who I am and not because of the cool things I can do for them. It's great to be appreciated, right? Even though as a parent, I have the power to make things happen for them, and they know this, it's heart-warming when they don't ask for it and just show love anyway. The funny thing about that is when they don't ask, it makes me want to do things for them anyway.

I can imagine that in some ways, God desires the same from us from time to time. Even though His Word tells us that all we have to do is ask, I'm sure there are times when He'd much rather just hear our adoration for Him instead of the endless requests.

I encourage you to spend a little time just showing God that you love Him for who He is and not because of what He can do for you. Sing praises. Offer prayers of thanksgiving. Simply adore Him.

Prayer: Heavenly Father, You are so worthy of praise. I praise You not because of what You can do for me but just because of who You are. Forgive me if I've ever allowed my desire for what You can do in my life to overshadow my love and adoration for You. May my praise bring joy to Your heart. In Jesus' name, Amen.

Further study: Psalm 34 and Psalm 150

The Life Your Spirit Craves for Mommies

Week 43 - Journal

~

When is the last time you spent time praising God just for who He is, without making a request?

_____
_____
_____
_____
_____

Are there times when your children simply shower you with love without asking for anything in return? How does that make you feel? How would this attitude warm the heart of God if you did the same?

_____
_____
_____
_____
_____
_____
_____
_____

Spend time this week, simply praising God for who He is. I think this shifts our focus a bit and reminds us of His glory and power. Did the time spent praising God have any impact on your growing relationship with Him this week?

_____
_____
_____
_____
_____
_____

Natasha D. Frazier

Week 44 - Memories

"Don't worry about anything; instead, pray about everything. Tell God what you need, and thank him for all he has done." (Philippians 4:6)

My daughter has a great memory! I'm not sure if it's because she's often reminding me about something I said or something that will benefit her in some way, but, nevertheless, she remembers all. When her teacher gives her a note to bring home, obviously the teacher tells the class what the note says because my daughter remembers every single detail, without having read the letter.

On two separate occasions, she brought home letters about something taking place at her school and the letter indicated what the parents needed to do to help make it happen. She reminded me every day until I took action. I don't need a calendar reminder when I have her.

I'm sure most of us were like this as children, remembering everything. But when did this end? Somewhere along the way, we lost our memory or at least pushed it into the back of our minds when it comes to God and all He has done for us. Why do we become so anxious when God has answered our prayers in the past? Why do we worry about whether or not God will take care of things on our behalf? Is it because we have forgotten His past performance in our lives? Do we need a memory refresher?

I encourage you to be anxious for nothing, but to remember who you know God to be and who His Word promises He will be. Search your memory for all that God has done for you and release your worry today.

Prayer: Heavenly Father, thank You for all that You've done for me. My memory isn't what it used to be, so some days I need little reminders that You are working on my behalf. Forgive me for my lack of faith. Help me to remember that Your grace is sufficient, Your Word never changes, and You are the same today as You were yesterday. I trust You. In Jesus' name, Amen.

Further study: Philippians 4:6–7; Matthew 6:25–34

The Life Your Spirit Craves for Mommies

Week 44 - Journal

~

Do you find yourself becoming anxious when waiting on God to answer your prayers? If so, why?

_____
_____
_____
_____
_____

Is there a prayer that you're currently waiting on God to answer? If so, what is it?

_____
_____
_____
_____
_____

Think of some recent prayers that God has answered and write them down as a reminder that God does hear and answer prayers. Sometimes the silence from God can cause us to become anxious and we forget that He is the same God and can do what He has done before in our lives - go before us and make our paths straight.

_____
_____
_____
_____
_____
_____

Natasha D. Frazier

Week 45 - Draw Near to God

"Come close to God, and God will come close to you. Wash your hands, you sinners; purify your hearts, for your loyalty is divided between God and the world." (James 4:8)

Every so often, we play a made-up game with the kids. It usually starts with something silly that will make them laugh and they ask to do it over and over again. It is now a game and it will last for as long as we allow it, because the kids are having such a great time.

I often wondered why is *this* silly game the thing they want to do when they have tons of toys and an outside playset? But then it dawned on me: It likely doesn't matter what we're doing as long as we're doing it together. It's all about the time spent and them knowing that they have our undivided attention. No TV, laptops, or phones getting in the way; they are the only ones who matter.

I wonder if it's the same with God. Whether we're praying, praising, studying, or meditating on His Word, does it bring Him joy? All of those things draw us closer to Him. Time in His presence is what He desires us to seek. He wants us to get to know Him more.

God deserves to be given a priority in our lives, so spending time in His presence is an absolute must. I encourage you to be intentional about how and when you spend time with God. Remember that He desires more of you.

Prayer: Heavenly Father, Your Word says that if I draw near to You that You will draw near to me. I desire to be close to You so I ask that You guide me in being intentional when it comes to my precious time with You. I want to grow into the woman of God You have designed me to be. In Jesus' name, Amen.

Further study: James 4:1–10

The Life Your Spirit Craves for Mommies

Week 45 - Journal

~

What is it that you do that helps you feel close to God?

_____
_____
_____
_____
_____
_____
_____

Are there times when you feel like you aren't close to God? Why? What is going on in your life during those times?

_____
_____
_____
_____
_____
_____
_____

What can you do to be closer to God this week? Do that each day this week and journal about the impact it has on your day.

_____
_____
_____
_____
_____
_____

Natasha D. Frazier

Week 46 - If You Love Me

"Love means doing what God has commanded us, and he has commanded us to love one another, just as you heard from the beginning." (2 John 6)

I went to visit with one of my friends who had a baby a few months ago. I had the kids in tow, so when we arrived, we sat in the car and I gave my speech about being on their best behavior and what would happen if they weren't. Smiles, nods, and a short round of *yes ma'am's* followed.

For the most part, they did well. However, there was a time when I had to take corrective action for the toddler jumping on my friend's couch and the older one not listening to instruction. After the visit, before returning to the car, my daughter ran toward me, threw her arms around me and said, "I love you, momma." At this point, I was mildly upset because I was thinking, *If you love me, you need to show it by doing what I tell you to do.*

That last statement hurts. Why? Because isn't that what God's Word instructs of us: If you love me, keep my commandments. Love has to be action. God demonstrated His love for us by sending His only Son to die for our sins. We have to show God we love Him by our obedience.

Perhaps we don't love God any less because of our disobedience, but our actions may say something different. Therefore, we must learn to show God we love Him by what we do out of love for Him. Consider how you feel when your children are disobedient yet they continue to request things of you. You love them, so you'll likely honor their request. In the same way, we as adults continue to approach the throne of God with numerous requests when our hearts are filled with sin. And God in all of His power continues to shower us with His love even when we're not honoring His Word. God is faithful to us even when we're unfaithful to Him. Shouldn't we at least honor Him by obeying His Word?

Prayer: Heavenly Father, thank You for the love that You continuously show me–unconditional love, not predicated on my actions. Teach me to honor Your Word so that I may teach my children to do the same. In Jesus' name, Amen.

Further study: John 14:23; 2 John 4–11

The Life Your Spirit Craves for Mommies

Week 46 - Journal

~

How do you feel when your children are disobedient but continue to request things of you? Do you think God may feel the same way about you?

_____
_____
_____
_____
_____
_____
_____

God's love is unconditional and it doesn't change when we are disobedient. How does this fact impact how you view your relationship with God and your children?

_____
_____
_____
_____
_____
_____
_____

Write a prayer asking God to help you show your love to Him through your obedience to his word.

_____
_____
_____
_____
_____
_____
_____

Natasha D. Frazier

Week 47 - God is Working

But Jesus replied, 'My Father is always working, and so am I.'" (John 5:17)

Dinner was ready. The kids were starving, as they are most days after I pick them up from school. I usually prepare their plates and set them aside to cool. Depending on the toddler's level of urgency, he may sample items off his plate before we all sit down to eat.

This particular night, I heard a few smacking sounds so I assumed that he was munching on a broccoli floret. I heard no whining; he was content and extremely quiet—except for the smacking. Silence is never good when it comes to him. I turned around from my busyness of preparing plates to see that he was not standing next to his high chair. I went into the living room to call them to the table and to my surprise, he was sitting on the floor, with his plate, eating and watching TV. He wasn't happy when I intervened, but we eventually made it to the table.

As I thought about how his silence is never a good sign, I was reminded of God's silence. His purposeful silence is just the opposite; it is an indicator that God is working on our behalf. In the midst of our frustration and need for immediate answers, we take silence from God as an indication that He isn't listening or He isn't moving. But just the opposite is true. God's Word reminds us that He is not limited by a special day, time, or space and that He is always working and so is Jesus.

Since God is always working, you can be confident and trust that His timing is perfect, no matter how it may seem.

Prayer: Heavenly Father, thank You for not operating on my schedule. Because of Your character and Your Word, I don't have to be anxious or worry that my prayers are not being answered. If I turn my heart to you and lay my requests at Your feet, You are faithful and just to do all that Your Word has declared. In Jesus' name, Amen.

Further study: John 5:16–30

The Life Your Spirit Craves for Mommies

Week 47 - Journal

~

How do you view God's silence?

_____
_____
_____
_____
_____
_____
_____
_____
_____

What actions do you take when God is silent?

_____
_____
_____
_____
_____
_____
_____
_____
_____

Think of a recent situation in which you were waiting on God to answer a prayer. In the midst of His silence, what did you do?

_____
_____
_____
_____
_____

Is there a prayer that you're still waiting on God to answer? To encourage yourself, write it here. Then write today's scripture next to it. When your prayer is answered, come back and write down how God answered your prayer.

The Life Your Spirit Craves for Mommies

Week 48 - A Thankful Heart

"And does the master thank the servant for doing what he was told to do? Of course not. In the same way, when you obey me you should say, 'We are unworthy servants who have simply done our duty.'" (Luke 17:9–10)

To encourage positive behavior, we started rewarding our kids with a piece of candy or something else they valued when they did a good job cleaning their rooms. The issue with this is that they now expect something in return for cleaning their rooms, doing homework, or doing anything they're told. The moment my daughter finishes a task and she is verbally complimented, she always asks for something in return for doing a *good job.* It's almost as if she thinks she's doing us a favor for doing what is required of her.

Some of that same type of behavior follows us into adulthood when it comes to our relationship with God. We obey God's Word and act as if we should receive a prize from God when in actuality, we are doing what God requires of us—our obedience to His Word. Any good thing that comes from our obedience shouldn't be an expectation, but we must understand that we have simply done our duty. If God shows us favor, then we should be grateful, but never have an attitude that something is owed to us in response to our submission to His Word.

Prayer: Heavenly Father, thank You for Your grace, mercy, and unmerited favor. Give me a heart to obey Your Word because of Your love for me. Let everything I do unto You be done with a pure heart. In Jesus' name, Amen.

Further study: Psalm 100

Week 48 - Journal

~

Do you believe that God has honored a prayer of yours in some way because of your obedience?

Do you expect some tangible thing or answered prayer from God when you're obedient to His word?

God shows us mercy and grace even when we don't deserve it. Whether or not you've been guilty of expecting God to do something for you in response to your obedience, write a prayer asking God to give you a grateful and willing heart to do what you've been called to do simply because His Word says so and not because you want something in return.

The Life Your Spirit Craves for Mommies

Week 49 - God's Gift

"For this is how God loved the world: He gave his one and only Son, so that everyone who believes in him will not perish but have eternal life." (John 3:16)

We typically celebrate Christmas in Mississippi with my family. This past Christmas, I decided I would let the children open a couple of gifts, which turned into all of their gifts, a couple of days before we took the trip. I'll admit that in the past, I have gone overboard purchasing gifts for them, but this past Christmas, I was committed to not going over budget and I'm proud to say that I did well.

Since my focus was on counting costs, many of the toys my daughter insisted that she wanted didn't make the cut. Considering she was only five years old, I didn't think it mattered. Besides, she wanted practically every toy advertised on TV. After they finished opening their gifts, she surprised me. She said thank you but not in the way she normally does. She squeezed my neck and held on for about a minute, and kissed my cheeks and exclaimed, "Mommy, thank you! This is just what I always wanted." She then repeated her actions of gratefulness to her dad. I was pretty convinced that she was grateful after such a display of affection.

That whole scene reminded me of God's gift to us: Jesus. Unlike us, God didn't hold back on his gift because of the cost; His gift to us is an expression of His love for us. What is it that we do to express our gratitude to God for His gift to us? He gives His gifts to us each day—grace, mercy, guidance, provision, love, peace, joy and so much more.

In or out of the Christmas season, let us commit to showing our gratitude to God for His Son Jesus, the One who gave His life so that we could have eternal life. Let us love God and one another the way God desires.

Prayer: Heavenly Father, thank You for each and every gift that You've given to us, especially Your Son Jesus. Thank You for being so generous with Your outpouring of love. Help me to see it each and every day and show love and kindness to others because You have done the same to me. In Jesus' name, Amen.

Further study: John 3

Week 49 - Journal

~

In what ways have you shown that you are grateful to God for His gift to you?

_____
_____
_____
_____
_____
_____
_____
_____

Has your child(ren) ever displayed affection toward you in such a way that reminded you to show gratitude to your Heavenly Father? What caused such gratefulness?

_____
_____
_____
_____
_____
_____
_____
_____

Write a prayer of thanks to God for His gifts to you. Also, ask God to help you spread the gift of His son Jesus to others.

_____
_____
_____
_____
_____
_____
_____
_____

The Life Your Spirit Craves for Mommies

Week 50 - Wearing Me Down

"The judge ignored her for a while, but finally he said to himself, 'I don't fear God or care about people, but this woman is driving me crazy. I'm going to see that she gets justice, because she is wearing me out with her constant requests!'" (Luke 18:4–5)

My daughter has the art of asking down pat. She's very persistent, and honestly, this can be annoying. I could be alone in this, but every now and again, I give in and say yes to that extra snack because it means that I'm going to have some sort of peace. It means that I won't have to hear the constant, "Momma, can I have . . . ?" Have you ever given in simply because you were tired of hearing your child ask?

In the Scripture text, the widow was persistent in requesting justice. In fact, the judge said that she was wearing him out and would drive him crazy if he didn't do anything about it. After Jesus told this parable, He said that if the judge who doesn't believe in God would respond to someone with such persistence, surely God would honor the one who is persistent and crying out to Him day and night. Persistent prayer and faith will move God.

Even when it seems that nothing is happening or God is silent, keep praying. Keep the faith. Your persistence shows God that you have faith in Him to act upon your request. Don't lose hope or become weary. Sometimes you just may have to be like a child or the persistent widow and ask until it is done.

Prayer: Heavenly Father, thank You for Your Word that reminds me to pray without ceasing and that You are faithful to answer. Keep me encouraged while I wait patiently on You. In Jesus' name, Amen.

Further study: Luke 18:1–8; Matthew 21:22; Matthew 7:7

Week 50 - Journal

~

Have you ever given in to your child's request simply because you were tired of hearing your child ask?

Have you ever been persistent in asking God for something as the widow in the text? Or do you simply give up if you haven't received an answer?

The Bible tells us that persistence shows God that we have enough faith in Him to act upon our request. If there is something that you've been praying about or have even given up asking about, write that prayer here. When God answers, come back and write His answer as a reminder to you of God's faithfulness.

The Life Your Spirit Craves for Mommies

Week 51 - Unconditional Love

"This is the message you have heard from the beginning: We should love one another." (1 John 3:11)

Before leaving for work, my husband always kisses the kids and me. One day, my daughter had done something that we had repeatedly told her not to do. My husband was frustrated and was going to walk out without giving her a kiss. She became sad and teary-eyed and I reminded him that he couldn't leave like that. She's five and won't be able to understand why "Daddy gave everyone else a kiss but me." I'm always conscious about their relationship because I believe that will have an impact on the type of guys she chooses to date and what she will or won't allow in her relationships when she gets older. He did turn around to kiss her, but also explained that he was disappointed in her.

That scene got me thinking. God loves us even when we do wrong and not only that, He continues to show it. He doesn't withhold His love from us when we disobey Him. We as His children have a problem with showing love even when someone else is wrong. What if something happened to my husband while he was out and that was my daughter's last time seeing him? What would her last impression have been? One thing that we work on is making sure that our children know that we still love them even when we don't approve of their behavior.

As brothers and sisters in Christ, we must learn to practice loving one another and showing it even when we've been wronged. I know it's hard to do, but will you join me in choosing to show love even when you don't feel like it? Christ loved us even when we were still in sin and showed that by giving His life.

Prayer: Heavenly Father, thank You for Your love that far exceeds my understanding. Help me to love past hurt. Teach me to love my brothers and sisters in a way that pleases You, and forgive me for the times when I haven't done so. In Jesus' name, Amen.

Further study: 1 John 3:11–24

Week 51 - Journal

~

Do you have issues showing love to those who have wronged you? Why or why not?

If you have problems with a loved one and have been holding a grudge, this is the week to get it right. Call that person and apologize, not because they have wronged you, but because you have not shown them the love that you should have, in spite of their wrong. Journal about the impact that has on your relationship with them and with God.

The Life Your Spirit Craves for Mommies

Week 52 - Children Are a Gift from God

"Children are a gift from the Lord; they are a reward from him." (Psalm 127:3)

Every so often I look at my children and I am amazed. I can recall the moment the pregnancy test read positive, the first ultrasound photo in which they looked like a small pea, pregnancy, the duration of labor, and how wonderful it felt to hold them against my chest for the first time. The experience is far beyond words and something I like to think about when they are not behaving like the gifts they are supposed to be.

Parenting is a role that I take seriously and feel honored that God has chosen me for such a task. And a task it is! There are times when I feel like being a parent is not a gift because of the difficult times, but I am reminded of today's Scripture and a lot of the lessons that I learn from my daily interaction from them.

No matter how you came to be a parent or how difficult the road may be, I encourage you to remember that children are God's gift. Just think about how they come to be. The entire process is amazing! Also know that we are God's children and He is like a father to us: full of love and compassion. Let God's love for you lead you in your parenting journey.

Prayer: Heavenly Father, thank You for the gift You've given me in my children. Help me to cherish and be a good steward over them, teaching them Your ways so that they may learn to love and follow You. Thank You for the reminders of Your love through them. In Jesus' name, Amen.

Further study: Psalm 127:3–4; Ephesians 5:1–2; Psalm 103:13

Week 52 - Journal

~

Can you recall the moment you learned that your children would come into your life? What was your response?

_____
_____
_____
_____
_____
_____
_____
_____
_____
_____

In what ways has being a parent helped you to become a stronger and better woman?

_____
_____
_____
_____
_____
_____
_____
_____
_____
_____

Write a prayer thanking God for choosing you to be a parent. Ask God to help you to remember the fact that you have been chosen, especially in difficult times.

The Life Your Spirit Craves for Mommies

Write a letter to your child(ren) expressing your love for them. (It doesn't have to be a letter that you will give them today; it can be given to them many years later or not at all. Perhaps it can serve as a reminder for you in difficult times. As you write, reflect on your love for them since the time they came into your life to the present.)

About the author

In addition to reading and writing, Natasha enjoys spending her time with her husband and children. She has won the Readers' Choice award for her books, _The Life Your Spirit Craves_ and _Love, Lies & Consequences_ at the Christian Literary Awards.

Natasha believes that we were all created for purpose and inspires women to pursue their God-given purpose through her books and the How Long Are You Going to Wait Conference. Sign up for her monthly newsletter at www.natashafrazier.com for encouraging devotionals, current events and new releases.